Biblical Entrepreneurship 40-Day Coaching Guide

A Spiritual Journey for Entrepreneurs and Marketplace Believers

---

Patrice Tsague

authorHOUSE®

AuthorHouse™
1663 Liberty Drive, Suite 200
Bloomington, IN 47403
www.authorhouse.com
Phone: 1-800-839-8640

First published by AuthorHouse 8/1/2008

ISBN: 978-1-4343-8234-4 (e)
ISBN: 978-1-4343-8236-8 (sc)

Library of Congress Control Number: 2008903956

Printed in the United States of America
Bloomington, Indiana

This book is printed on acid-free paper.

Dedication

This book is dedicated to all current and future Biblical Entrepreneurs

Special Thanks

Very special thanks to my Lord and Savior Jesus Christ for forgiving me, saving me, teaching me and guiding me to the purpose and destiny He has for me. Special thanks to my wife Gina Tsague and my two children Gabrielle and Danielle, for supporting me and loving me unconditionally. Thank you to all who contributed to the release of this book: Glenn Repple for your encouragement, guidance and support; the G.A. Repple Family for your support of NPIM; Art Ally and the Timothy Plan for your support of NPIM; Gloria Shunda for being a super office manager and all of your editing work; all of my copy editors: Kevin Greene, Janice McMillian, Melvin Mooring (II) , Maret Reynolds, and Steve Sappington for your assistance in reviewing the manuscript; the NPIM Board of Directors, Wall Builders, and Legacy Partners for sustaining the vision; and last but not least Bishop Johnson and First Lady Chrys Johnson for your spiritual leadership, and the Bethel World Outreach Church Family for your love and support.

Contents

Foreword

I entered business as a secular entrepreneur in 1982 and later was transformed into a Biblical Entrepreneur. This change took time and has been a continual process. The marketplace is a laboratory of life that has tested and changed me. In the marketplace we quickly learn about stewardship and ownership; that God owns everything in the heavens and in the earth. He is the Creator and Author of life.

In the marketplace you are challenged to compromise your values daily. Your character is tested through relationships, employees, and through dealing with issues involving staff, service, vendors, finances and products. You will fall and get back up. You will experience betrayal, gossip, envy, jealously, pride, arrogance, greed, dishonesty and disloyalty. As a Biblical Entrepreneur you will also experience love, forgiveness, joy, growth, peace, change, renewal, patience, fulfillment and greater responsibility as a reward for being a steward over God's resources. Your character will be shaped and molded by every experience and test. You will be broken and then put back together. You will be hurt but you will forgive. You will be taken advantage of but you will smile in love. You will learn to serve rather than be served as Jesus taught and exemplified through the giving of His life.

One of the greatest spiritual disciplines that have helped me throughout my entrepreneurial journey has been having a quiet time every day. Over the years the amount of time I spend in the morning has increased from 15 minutes to sometimes as much as 2 hours. There seems to be a direct correlation between my attitude and the time I spend in worship daily.

Jesus said, "I am the way, the truth and the life…" If we want to know God's ways we need to spend time with HIM. We need to read His Word. We need to earnestly seek Him. If we want to know truth, we need to spend time with the Author of truth. If we want to experience life to the fullest, we need to seek the presence of Jesus Christ on a daily basis. This comes by spending time with Him daily, with our hearts and minds open to receive His Word. Then we can walk in His ways, knowing His truth and experiencing the abundant life.

I encourage you to take up this 40–day challenge. Open up your mind and heart to receive coaching that will change your thinking and renew your mind. Commit to reading a session each day and studying God's Word for 30 minutes. Change comes with the renewal of your mind. Your thinking must change for your beliefs to change. Change needs to occur in your mind and heart so that your actions will follow. Take the 40–day challenge to renew your mind and become transformed into a Biblical Entrepreneur.

Glenn Repple
Founder and President, G.A. Repple & Company

G.A. Repple & Company is a comprehensive, independent, and objective FULL SERVICE investment and securities firm. Founded in 1982, we distribute our services through more than 60 independently owned branch offices nationally. G. A. Repple & Company is a registered Broker Dealer and Registered Investment Advisor. The heart of G. A. Repple & Company is in our desire to make a positive cultural change in the world. We provide planned giving services for "non profit" organizations and their ministries. We are able to provide our clients with the ability to manage their client's monies with moral responsibility. We have helped fund and build over 80 Churches, set up 200 foundations and raised over $100,000,000 for various ministries, Churches and foundations.

It is our vision to see Advisors transforming communities across the country through work place ministry. We see Advisors impacting their communities by teaching Biblical Stewardship and Biblical Entrepreneurship. We see Advisors providing Godly financial counsel. We would like to see every Church and ministry with a Stewardship Minister. We would like to see every Church and Ministry with an endowment or foundation.

G. A. Repple & Company
101 Normandy Road
Casselberry, FL 32707
866 373 7753

Introduction

I am so excited about the release of this daily devotional book because it speaks to an area of our lives that is so critical to our development as Biblical Entrepreneurs; the importance of taking time daily to pray and meditate upon scripture and its application to our business life.

In Mark 1:35, we learn that Jesus rose before daylight to go to a solitary place to pray before starting His day. I believe that is a model we all have to follow if we are to experience the abundant life that He promised. Of course these were not the only times that Jesus spent with His Father. There are several examples of when He took time during the day to go to a mountain for prayer. Jesus understood that if His ministry was to be successful, it could not depend on His natural talents or abilities but on His relationship with the Father. I believe most Biblical Entrepreneurs understand that too. That is why for years many people have asked me to publish a devotional for entrepreneurs; a book that could serve as a guide to those who desire to seek the wisdom of God in various areas of business, and provide patterns of prayer and ways that the information can be applied to their business lives. This devotional book is our first edition. It is a compilation of 40 weeks of our devotional e-mails that go out weekly to hundreds of entrepreneurs around the world. Each day includes a scripture of the day, information on a specific topic based on the scripture of the day, a prayer pattern based on the information, and an application. The application is designed to assist you in applying the information that you just read. We do not want you to just read the information. We want you to make a commitment to apply what you have learned. We also provide you with a comment section to write down any insights the Lord gives you while you are studying.

This devotional can also serve as a tool to journal your interactions with your Father, your prayer requests, your weekly commitments, and the insights He reveals to you. My prayer is that you will actively use this devotional book to assist you, in the next 40 days, to get closer to your Father and to fulfill His plans for your life through business. If you are a Biblical Entrepreneur alumnus or currently subscribe to our weekly e-mail devotional, I thank you for being a part of the Biblical Entrepreneurship family and for your commitment to being the salt and light of the marketplace. If you have not yet taken the Biblical Entrepreneurship Certificate Program, I encourage you to visit our website www.nehemiahproject.org and register today. We offer both live and online classes. Do not forget to sign up for our E-devotionals so you can get additional weekly business insights based on the Bible. We also encourage you to stay up to date with our development and the various opportunities available through the Nehemiah Project International Ministries, Inc. which will help you fulfill God's plan for your life through business.

God bless you!

Patrice Tsague
Chief Servant Officer, NPIM

Day 1

CALLED TO BE IN THE MARKETPLACE

...Then Jesus said to Simon, "Don't be afraid from now on you will catch men." So they pulled their boats up on shore, left everything and followed him. **Luke 5:10-11**

Too often we as Christians have two lives: our church life, where we do our so-called ministry, and our secular life, where we earn our living. If we feel called into what we consider to be full-time ministry, the immediate assumption is that we are called to be the traditional Pastor who must establish a local church. Many have even left their businesses or professions in the marketplace thinking that the only way to be in full-time ministry is to be a part of the local church staff or be involved in foreign missions, only to find themselves outside of the will of God. Ministry is bigger than the local church; ministry involves every aspect of our society. There are three basic institutions that God has established where ministry must be carried out: the local church, the family, and the marketplace. Among those institutions, the marketplace is the one where we spend most of our time with the majority of unsaved people. Marketplace ministry challenges those of us who spend much of our time in the marketplace to accept our call into full time ministry. It challenges us to allow Jesus Christ to change us from fishermen to *fishers of men*. Many of us who have accepted Christ are still acting as fishermen. We spend most of our time and energy in the marketplace toiling and worrying about how much fish we can catch, not realizing that we are no longer fishermen but fishers of men. As fishers of men Jesus has now taken the responsibility to ensure that we catch enough fish to make our business profitable, our project successful, or that our campaign for office prevails. Are you a fisherman or a fisher of men? I started my career as an entrepreneurship instructor, executive director, and founder of a nonprofit youth organization. I was doing good works according to most standards: providing

❧ BE Thought of the Day

There are three basic institutions that God has established where ministry must be carried out; the local church, the family and the marketplace.

leadership training to young aspiring leaders and helping young people learn the skills of business so they could have an alternative to drugs. But in 1995, through a Christian businessman who was operating in his marketplace ministry, I received the Lord Jesus Christ as my Savior. That led to a personal transformation where I received my call to use entrepreneurship as a tool to empower the body of Christ and to seek and save the lost. That revelation then led me to develop an entrepreneurship training program called Biblical Entrepreneurship and to restructure the organization my wife and I founded into a service ministry called Nehemiah Project International Ministries. This ministry helps people fulfill God's plan for their lives through business by working with businesses, churches, parachurch ministries, and Christian colleges and universities. At that moment I went from being a fisherman to being a fisher of men. Your transition may not be as drastic; it may not even cause you to change what you are doing. You may only have to change the way you do things and your attitude towards doing them. By the grace of God, the Lord has blessed us to assist hundreds of individuals who are now fulfilling God's plan for their lives in the marketplace. Many are even making money doing so.

BE Prayer of the Day

Father, please give me the wisdom to identify my marketplace ministry and the courage to carry it out with boldness, representing You as Your ambassador in this arena, in Jesus' name, Amen.

BE Application of the Day

- Do you know God's plan for your life?
- How are you carrying it out in your family, in your local church, and in the marketplace?

_____

_____

_____

_____

_____

_____

_____

_____

_____

_____

_____

_____

_____

_____

_____

- Reflect on these passages of scripture and explain how they relate to today's devotional: Jeremiah 1:4-10 and Romans 8:28-30.

_____

_____

_____

_____

_____

_____

_____

_____

_____

_____

_____

_____

Day 2
ARE YOU A BIBLICAL ENTREPRENEUR?

Who may ascend the hill of the Lord? Who may stand in his holy place? He who has clean hands and a pure heart, who does not lift up his soul to an idol or swear by what is false.
Psalm 24:3-4

Biblical Entrepreneurship is a biblically-based process of identifying opportunities, taking calculated risks, solving problems, and exercising business stewardship for profit. In Biblical Entrepreneurship, the Bible is your guide and everything you do is based on the Word of God. This ensures that you remain in the will of God as you go through the process of using your gifts, skills and treasures in business. As you identify opportunities, assess these qualities and serve your community by providing goods or services, you must keep your mind focused on the One who has given you those qualities and called you to be in business. Once you have identified your opportunity, you will take calculated risks by counting the cost of taking advantage of the opportunity you have identified. Additionally, you will develop a plan to actualize it. Biblical Entrepreneurship is about solving problems. The opportunity you identify will be a problem encountered by people in your church, community or nation. You, in turn, can find or develop a product or service to solve this problem. As you solve the problems you may encounter, you will be exercising stewardship over a business.

We use the phrase "exercising business stewardship" instead of "owning a business" because the business does not belong to you; it belongs to the Lord. You are only a steward over it. As you exercise business stewardship, you will generate a profit. Whenever you exercise good stewardship over something, a profit is generated. However, this should not be your sole motivation for going into business. Your primary focus should be to serve people

> 𝒫 BE Thought of the Day
>
> Biblical Entrepreneurship is a biblically-based process of identifying opportunities, taking calculated risks, solving problems, and exercising business stewardship for profit.

5

through your products and services. In Biblical Entrepreneurship, profit is the fruit, not the goal of good stewardship. Moreover, Biblical Entrepreneurs profit both spiritually and financially because the profit is the result of good stewardship and obedience to God's Word.

BE Prayer of the Day

Father, I ask you to open my eyes to see the business opportunities that are available to me. Give me the grace to effectively exercise stewardship over the business you give me, in Jesus' name, Amen.

BE Application of the Day

- Have you identified your opportunity?
- What is the cost of taking advantage of the opportunity you have identified?
- What product or service could you create or use?
- How can you exercise stewardship over a business?

_____
_____
_____
_____
_____
_____
_____
_____
_____
_____
_____
_____

- Reflect on these passages of scripture and explain how they relate to today's devotional: Ecclesiastes 9:10 and Colossians 3:23.

_____
_____
_____
_____
_____
_____
_____
_____
_____
_____
_____
_____
_____

$Day\ 3$
IDENTIFYING OPPORTUNITIES

So Pharaoh asked them, "Can we find anyone like this man, one in whom is the spirit of God?" Then Pharaoh said to Joseph, "Since God has made all this known to you, there is no one so discerning and wise as you. You shall be in charge of my palace, and all my people are to submit to your orders. Only with respect to the throne will I be greater than you." So Pharaoh said to Joseph, "I hereby put you in charge of the whole land of Egypt." Then Pharaoh took his signet ring from his finger and put it on Joseph's finger. He dressed him in robes of fine linen and put a gold chain around his neck. He had him ride in a chariot as his second-in-command, and men shouted before him, "Make way!" Thus he put him in charge of the whole land of Egypt. **Genesis 41:38-4**

Entrepreneurial success begins with opportunity recognition. Most people spend their time chasing after opportunities, believing that their big hit is just an opportunity away. The problem with this approach is that they often are unprepared for the opportunity they find. They may find themselves lured into the wrong kind of opportunity, which ends up being an opportunity for someone else and a disaster for themselves. In Biblical Entrepreneurship, we believe that opportunities are found in the midst of problems. **Identifying opportunities** is recognizing when the timing of God meets preparation. This principle helps you recognize God's timing for getting into business, starting a particular business, or expanding an existing business. It requires that you know your abilities, and that you cooperate with God in developing them. It also requires that you recognize beneficial gain in the midst of circumstances that may seem less than advantageous. While Joseph was in Egypt, God used various circumstances such as slavery and prison to prepare him for the opportunity that was to come. When his opportunity came, it was disguised as a problem (in this case a famine). Because he was prepared, he was able to provide a solution and to manage the project Pharaoh asked him to manage. Whenever the timing of God meets preparation, an opportunity presents itself. As you believe God for the right

> ✍ BE Thought of the Day
>
> Identifying opportunities is recognizing when the timing of God meets preparation.

9

opportunity for you, focus on preparing yourself for it instead of chasing it and, learn how to discern God's will so you will be able to identify it when it comes.

BE Prayer of the Day

Father, I pray for the grace to prepare for the opportunities that will come my way. I also pray that I will discern the seasons of my life so that I will know when the opportunity arises, in Jesus' name, Amen.

BE Application of the Day

- Are you preparing for opportunities or chasing after them?
- What opportunities can you find in the midst of problems?

_____

_____

_____

_____

_____

_____

_____

_____

_____

_____

_____

_____

_____

_____

_____

_____

- Reflect on these passages of scripture and explain how they relate to today's devotional: 1 Samuel 17: 33-35 and Esther 4:14.

_____

_____

_____

_____

_____

_____

_____

_____

_____

_____

_____

_____

_____

_____

Day 4

TAKING CALCULATED RISKS

Suppose one of you wants to build a tower. Will he not first sit down and estimate the cost to see if he has enough money to complete it? **Luke 14:28**

Once you have identified an opportunity within your business or God's plan for your life, a risk will be present. The greater the opportunity is, the greater the risks will be. **Taking Calculated Risks** entail counting all the costs involved to ensure that there are adequate resources available to finish the task. This principle helps you reduce your risk of failure and ensures that you are spiritually, naturally, mentally, and emotionally prepared to start and operate a successful, effective business. Successful entrepreneurs are not those who take the most amount of risk. Rather they are the ones who minimize their risks. There are various ways in which you can prepare yourself to minimize risk, including the following:

- **Spiritual preparation** – Going before God in prayer and fasting based on the magnitude of the opportunity.

- **Natural preparation** – Developing a business plan, assessing the magnitude of the problem, remaining under the appropriate authorities, and gathering all of the resources that you need.

- **Mental and emotional preparation** – this is the most critical level of preparation. Since business is a long-term proposition, you have to have the mental toughness to endure the ups and downs and trials that you will face along the way. Therefore, you must guard your mind and heart against discouragement and negativity, and be focused on finishing what you have begun.

> ✌ BE Thought of the Day
>
> Taking calculated risks entail counting all the costs involved to ensure that there are adequate resources available to finish the task.

BE Prayer of the Day

Father, I ask for the courage I need to take risks. Help me to prepare enough so that I can minimize the risks I will have to take, and to be committed enough to stick with the business in tough times, in Jesus' name, Amen.

BE Application of the Day

- What are you doing to minimize your risk?
- In what ways are you preparing yourself spiritually, naturally, mentally and emotionally?
- Do you have the perseverance and determination to stick with the business in tough times?

_____
_____
_____
_____
_____
_____
_____
_____
_____
_____
_____
_____
_____

- Reflect on these passages of scripture and explain how they relate to today's devotional: Proverbs 24:27 and Ecclesiastes 11:1.

_____
_____
_____
_____
_____
_____
_____
_____
_____
_____
_____
_____
_____

Day 5

SOLVING PROBLEMS

Do not be anxious about anything, but in everything, by prayer and petition, with thanksgiving, present your requests to God. And the peace of God, which transcends all understanding, will guard your hearts and your minds in Christ Jesus. **Philippians 4:6-7**

The hallmark of successful entrepreneurs is their ability to master the art of problem solving. Contrary to popular opinion, the art of problem solving is not finding the solution, but finding a place of peace. You may find the solution without finding peace, but if you can find peace, you will eventually find the solution. The principle of problem solving is coming into agreement with the Word of God. Therein you will find the solution to any situation that presents a need, uncertainty, or difficulty. Whether you are facing market problems, industry problems, administrative and management problems, or spiritual problems, this principle will enable you to keep the challenges of operating a business from stealing your peace. No matter the circumstance, you can find the answer in the Word of God. You may not be able to identify an immediate solution, but you will always receive an immediate peace if you believe. Remember, peace is not the absence of problems but rather, the result of an internal confidence and trust in the perfect will of God for your life. This manifestation cultivates an external confidence that gives you assurance in everything you do.

> ✍ BE Thought of the Day
>
> …peace is not the absence of problems but rather, the result of an internal confidence and trust in the perfect will of God for your life.

BE Prayer of the Day

Father, I bring the problems that are confronting me before You. I pray that Your peace will overwhelm me as I choose to trust in Your Word, in Jesus' name, Amen.

BE Application of the Day

- What kinds of problems are you facing?
- Look to the Word of God to find the sense of peace that you need.

_____

_____

_____

_____

_____

_____

_____

_____

_____

_____

_____

_____

_____

_____

_____

- Reflect on these passages of scripture and explain how they relate to today's devotional: Isaiah 26:3 and Daniel 5: 11-12.

_____

_____

_____

_____

_____

_____

_____

_____

_____

_____

_____

_____

Course Information Sheet

KZMB10 / MGT-539

Course: Entrepreneurship and Innovation

Faculty Member: Taylor, Jeannette Louise

Course Description:

A focused study of the tools needed in identifying and capitalizing on entrepreneurial business opportunities, methods for managing those opportunities and critical thinking skills needed for innovation and growth. Students work with a team to design an entrepreneurial venture. Additional topics include how to stimulate new ideas, managing innovative ideas, adapting to change and the individual's and group's role in the creative process.

Dates: 2/3/2015, 2/10/2015, 2/17/2015, 2/24/2015, 3/3/2015, 3/17/2015

Night: Tuesday

Time: 6:00PM

Location: West Pointe Centre #1080 2

Home Phone: 616-285-6898

Email: jeannette.taylor@cornerstone.edu

If you have any questions concerning your class, please contact your instructor. A complete syllabus will be distributed the first night of class.

*Note to Online students — The dates listed indicate when weekly assignments are to be completed. The course will be available in Moodle to begin work approximately one week prior to the first date listed. Some elements of the assignments for the first week may be due during the week prior to the first date listed.

Note: The University will make reasonable accommodations for students with disabilities in accordance with the statement found in the Professional && Graduate Studies Academic Catalog.

Day 6

BUSINESS STEWARDSHIP

O LORD, our Lord, how majestic is your name in all the earth! You have set your glory above the heavens. From the lips of children and infants you have ordained praise because of your enemies, to silence the foe and the avenger. When I consider your heavens, the work of your fingers, the moon and the stars, which you have set in place, what is man that you are mindful of him, the son of man that you care for him? You made him a little lower than the heavenly beings and crowned him with glory and honor. You made him ruler over the works of your hands; you put everything under his feet: all flocks and herds, and the beasts of the field, the birds of the air, and the fish of the sea, all that swim the paths of the seas. O LORD, our Lord, how majestic is your name in all the earth!
Psalms 8:1-9

Had Adam not sinned, there would be no need for business commerce because there would be free distribution of God's resources. Business stewardship began with God instructing Adam in Genesis 1:15 to dress and keep the garden. Until that time, God's idea of stewardship precluded commerce, since Adam was free to eat of any tree of the garden except the tree of the knowledge of good and evil. Sin is what introduced commerce into the whole idea of stewardship. Once Adam sinned against God, the punishment was severe. Genesis 3:17-19 states, *"...cursed is the ground because of you; through painful toil you will eat of it all the days of your life. It will produce thorns and thistles for you, and you will eat the plants of the field. By the sweat of your brow you will eat your food until you return to the ground, since from it you were taken; for dust you are and to dust you will return."* This meant that from that day forward, everyone had to earn his or her own provision.

Business stewardship then, is taking dominion over the natural resources of God in order to serve others, while simultaneously making a profit for the Kingdom of God. This principle helps you recognize the fact that you own nothing. All that you have (the gifts, skills, treasure, business ideas, and the business) belongs

> ✍ BE Thought of the Day
>
> Business stewardship...is taking dominion over the natural resources of God in order to serve others, while simultaneously making a profit for the Kingdom of God.

to the Lord Jesus Christ. We are only temporary stewards of His goods. Through business stewardship, we are able to make provisions for our needs and the needs of others.

BE Prayer of the Day

Father, thank you for the business You have given me to steward. Help me to remember that everything I have belongs to You and to use all the resources You have given me to further Your kingdom, in Jesus' name, Amen.

BE Application of the Day

- What has been your mindset with respect to ownership?
- Realize that ultimately God owns everything and seek to be a good steward over His resources.

_____

_____

_____

_____

_____

_____

_____

_____

_____

_____

_____

_____

_____

_____

_____

- Reflect on these passages of scripture and explain how they relate to today's devotional: Proverbs 27:23 and I Timothy 6:6-7.

_____

_____

_____

_____

_____

_____

_____

_____

_____

_____

_____

_____

_____

_____

Day 7

BIBLICAL PROFIT

But godliness with contentment is great gain. **I Timothy 6:6**

Profit is the most misunderstood term in the business world. The greedy capitalist feels that profit is the reward of being an entrepreneur and that the goal of business is to maximize profit no matter the cost. Many Christians are afraid of profit and even misquote I Timothy 6:10 by saying, "money is a root of all kinds of evil…" They ignore the fact that the scripture actually states, *"the love of money is a root of all kinds of evil…"* Some may even argue that it all depends on which Bible translation you use. Whatever your belief, Jesus is very clear in the parable of the talents on how He views profit. He cast the unprofitable servant into outer darkness. He also stated in Proverbs 16:8 that *"better is little with righteousness than great revenues without right"* (KJV). Therefore as Biblical Entrepreneurs, we have a responsibility to be profitable, but we must do it within the guidelines of the Word of God. Just as it does not please God when we profit through ungodly means, God is equally not pleased when we do not profit because of fear or a lack of proper stewardship. **Biblical Profit** is the spiritual and natural gain that remains after all costs are deducted from a business transaction or from the total income of the business. As a Biblical Entrepreneur, you must profit both spiritually and naturally.

> ✍ BE Thought of the Day
>
> Biblical Profit is the spiritual and natural gain that remains after all costs are deducted from a business transaction or from the total income of the business.

BE Prayer of the Day

Father, I know that it is Your will that my business be profitable. I pray for the knowledge I need to generate profits and the wisdom to do so based on Your Word, in Jesus' name, Amen.

BE Application of the Day

- What is your view of profit? Is your view biblical?
- Seek biblical guidelines for how you can generate profit.

_____
_____
_____
_____
_____
_____
_____
_____
_____
_____
_____
_____
_____
_____

- Reflect on these passages of scripture and explain how they relate to today's devotional: Proverbs 21:5 and Proverbs 30:7-9.

_____
_____
_____
_____
_____
_____
_____
_____
_____
_____
_____
_____
_____

Day 8

WHAT IS PLANNING?

See that you make them according to the pattern shown you on the mountain. **Exodus 25:40**

Planning is the ability to tap into the mind of God and gather the necessary details on how the vision He gave you will be implemented. It requires you to do careful research so you can effectively support and communicate the assumptions you make throughout the plan based upon the revelations that the Lord has given you.

Planning is essential to the success of any business. It is key to not only start the business, but to manage the business as well. Can you imagine Moses building the tabernacle of God without a plan from God? Or Jesus fulfilling His purpose on the earth without the blueprints of the Old Testament to make references to and be guided by? Effective management begins with planning, which leads to setting goals. Planning is the most important function in establishing a business. The sad reality is that most entrepreneurs do not bother to plan. They may think they lack the time, the know-how, or they may just feel it is not necessary. Without a doubt, planning involves thinking, and thinking is hard work. Effective planning includes the following: solving future problems before they occur, making decisions, speculating on the future (both far and near), setting objectives (long and short range), considering alternatives, and making choices. Planning for the future requires flexibility to cope with the unexpected. You must set timetables and establish priorities, decide on the methods to be used and the people who will be involved. You must analyze the existing situation, formulate and apply targets, logic, and creativity to all details during the process. Planning gives purpose and direction to your daily activities. Without it, your activities are

&? BE Thought of the Day

Planning gives purpose and direction to your daily activities. Without it, your activities are aimless and uncoordinated.

29

aimless and uncoordinated. Whether you are a start-up business or a growing business, if you have not developed a plan, it is essential that you do so, not just for your sake, but for the sake of those who are called to co-labor with you.

Eliminate the excuses, overcome the procrastination, discipline yourself, and write your plan. Just doing it will be a reward in itself.

BE Prayer of the Day

Father, I pray that you grant me the grace to plan effectively for my business, and I ask that You would bless those plans and enable me to implement them, in Jesus' name, Amen.

BE Application of the Day

- What are your excuses for not planning?
- Overcome those obstacles and write your plan.

_____

_____

_____

_____

_____

_____

_____

_____

_____

_____

_____

_____

_____

- Reflect on these passages of scripture and explain how they relate to today's devotional: Habakkuk 2:2-3 and 1 Chronicles 28: 11-13.

_____

_____

_____

_____

_____

_____

_____

_____

_____

_____

_____

_____

_____

Day 9

COUNT IT ALL JOY

My brethren, count it all joy when ye fall into divers temptations; knowing this, that the trying of your faith worketh patience. But let patience have her perfect work, that ye may be perfect and entire, wanting nothing. **James 1:2-4 (KJV)**

It was 2002. I was anxious to leave an organization I was a part of because it became clear to me that although I began my spiritual journey there, that was not where it would end. Also, I was angry because I felt I had been mistreated. As I prepared to leave, I did something I always do before making any major decision. I prayed, sought the council of others I respected, and then I went to the Lord again for final confirmation. The answer the Lord gave me was, "Count it all joy and allow your trials to work patience in you so you may be complete lacking nothing." I asked, "Lord how will I know when I am complete and lack for nothing?" He said to me, "When your conversation changes." You see, out of the abundance of the heart, the mouth speaks. I was hurt and hurt was coming out of me. Had I left then, I would have been a hurt person who would later hurt others. I have discovered that people who are hurting tend to hurt others who in turn hurt more people and the cycle continues. The Lord's instruction to count it all joy was the best advice I received, and it has led to great fruit later in my development.

Counting it all joy means that you maintain an internal peace with an external praise that passes all of your understanding. No matter the circumstance, you realize that God will work all things together for your good and that are *"the sufferings of this present time is not worthy to be compared with the glory which shall be revealed in [you]"* Romans 8:18 (KJV). The trial of your faith is working patience in you. **Patience** is doing what you can while waiting on God to do what only He can.

> ℘ BE Thought of the Day
>
> Count it all joy because God is taking you somewhere and the greater the suffering, the greater the reward; the greater the sacrifice, the greater the fruit.

Patience is God's plan to give you everything that you desire within His season which is in line with His plan for your life. Patience is produced through trials, and we need patience to have character, because without character we have no hope. Hope is essential to realizing our business and personal goals and objectives.

Allowing patience to be complete in us allows us to be complete on the inside and outside, lacking nothing. God wants us to be whole. He wants us to completely depend on Him and on Him alone. He wants us to have life and have it more abundantly. In order for us to achieve complete internal wholeness and walk in the abundant life, God first allows us to go through trials and tribulations. Count it all joy because God is taking you somewhere and the greater the suffering, the greater the reward; the greater the sacrifice, the greater the fruit. As you endure trials, you will need wisdom from God to handle them. He will give you wisdom to handle even the most difficult circumstances. It has been five years since the Lord gave me the instructions to count it all joy. As I look back, I am so thankful that I obeyed Him. Had I not obeyed Him, I would have shipwrecked His purpose and plan for my life. No matter how difficult or challenging your trials may be, my advice to you is to count it all joy. Remember the Apostle Paul who, while in prison, wrote these words to us in Philippians 4:4-7: *"Rejoice in the Lord always. I will say it again: Rejoice! Let your gentleness be evident to all. The Lord is near. Do not be anxious about anything, but in everything, by prayer and petition, with thanksgiving, present your requests to God. And the peace of God, which transcends all understanding, will guard your hearts and your minds in Christ Jesus."*

BE Prayer of the Day

Father, help me to count it all joy no matter what circumstance I am experiencing. Help me to trust that You are working all things for my good, in Jesus' name, Amen.

BE Application of the Day

- What trials have you gone through or are you going through right now that are causing you great internal pain? Count it all joy.
- Have customers and employees disappointed you lately? Count it all joy.
- Have you been mistreated by those you love the most? Count it all joy.

_____

_____

_____

_____

_____

_____

_____

_____

_____

_____

- Reflect on these passages of scripture and explain how they relate to today's devotional: 2 Corinthians 4:16-18 and Hebrews 12:1-2.

_____

_____

_____

_____

_____

_____

_____

_____

_____

_____

_____

_____

_____

Day 10

THE PURSUIT OF HAPPINESS

Blessed are those who hunger and thirst for righteousness, for they will be filled.
Matthew 5:6

The American Declaration of Independence includes this famous line: "We hold these truths to be self-evident, that all men are created equal, that they are endowed by their Creator with certain unalienable Rights, that among these are Life, Liberty and <u>the pursuit of Happiness</u>." One may argue that the term "the pursuit of happiness" is the fuel behind our materialistic society. Since many entrepreneurs are pursuing happiness, they believe that they have the right to anything that will make them happy. The Bible teaches about happiness within the context that it is a divine favor from God as a result of our obedience to His Word. The biblical term for it is "bless". In His Sermon on the Mountain, or the Beatitudes, Jesus said blessed or happy are the poor in spirit, blessed are those who mourn, blessed are the meek, and blessed are those who hunger and thirst for righteousness, etc (Matthew 5:3-6). We can conclude that God does want us to be happy, but this happiness is the by-product of a spiritual pursuit and not the end in itself. Happiness is not guaranteed. It is a reward to those who do the will of the Father. Happiness is not a result of our efforts and ingenuity, but the result of divine favor. How do biblical entrepreneurs pursue this happiness? This happiness is achieved by acquiring the following spiritual attributes: poor in spirit (recognition of our spiritual poverty before God. We realize that we are in complete need of Him, only He can enrich our lives, and without Him we are miserable); mourning (to have a feeling of grief; we must not be too proud but rather grieve before God for the unrighteousness around us, so He may bring us comfort); meekness (power under control; we must not use our advantage or talents to advance our own agenda but rather to protect and defend others); hungering and thirsting after righteousness (we must demonstrate a continuous strong

> **✍ BE Thought of the Day**
>
> Happiness is a divine favor from God as a result of our obedience to His Word.

desire for God and the Word of God); mercy (we must demonstrate compassion toward others, especially those who are suffering); pure at heart (having a singleness of focus before God and allowing His word to transform us on the inside); peacemakers (we must make an attempt to bring harmony and reconciliation to those that are estranged. We must strive to build harmony between others and not discord); and being persecuted for righteousness' sake (allowing ourselves to suffer in the hands of those who do not know nor understand our Savior and His plan for our lives). Matthew 5:3-12 tells us:

Blessed are the poor in spirit,
*   for theirs is the kingdom of heaven.*
Blessed are those who mourn,
*   for they will be comforted.*
Blessed are the meek,
*   for they will inherit the earth.*
Blessed are those who hunger and thirst for righteousness,
*   for they will be filled.*
Blessed are the merciful,
*   for they will be shown mercy.*
Blessed are the pure in heart,
*   for they will see God.*
Blessed are the peacemakers,
*   for they will be called sons of God.*
Blessed are those who are persecuted because of righteousness,
*   for theirs is the kingdom of heaven.*
Blessed are you when people insult you, persecute you and falsely say all
kinds of evil against you because of me
Rejoice and be glad, because great is your reward in heaven, for in the
same way they persecuted the prophets who were before you.

Do you still want to be happy? If so, covet after these things and happiness will be yours.

BE Prayer of the Day

Father, I thank You for the joy that I have in a personal relationship with Your Son Jesus. Help me to seek my happiness in You, rather than in material things, people or my achievements. In Jesus' name, Amen.

BE Application of the Day

- Where do you find your happiness?
- Identify key things about your relationship with the Lord that brings you happiness.

_____
_____
_____
_____
_____
_____
_____
_____
_____
_____
_____
_____
_____
_____

- Reflect on these passages of scripture and explain how they relate to today's devotional: Proverbs 16:20 and Ecclesiastes 2: 1-11, 24-26.

_____
_____
_____
_____
_____
_____
_____
_____
_____
_____
_____
_____
_____
_____

Day 11

LET PATIENCE HAVE HER PERFECT WORK

But let patience have her perfect work, that ye may be perfect and entire, wanting nothing. **James 1:4 (KJV)**

Patience is not an attribute that you find very common among entrepreneurs, since the common thinking in the business world is that time is money and that we only have 24 hours in a day. So we have to hurry up and trade everything we have for money before our time runs out. After all, the Bible teaches us to redeem the time. This mindset influences many Biblical entrepreneurs to enter the rat race. I find myself guilty of this when I forsake my spiritual and familial responsibilities because of the deadlines and the goals I think I have to meet, only to find myself never catching up and losing my internal balance.

Patience is a virtue. It is a fruit of the Spirit and the lack of it demonstrates a lack of spiritual maturity. Impatient people are an accident waiting to happen. Impatient people put themselves above the laws of God and man. Impatient people cheat, get speeding tickets, jump in line, lie on their taxes, curse at their children, and the list goes on. Impatient people eventually lack integrity because they focus more on the outcome than the process. Impatient people take matters into their own hands instead of waiting on God. Without patience, you will never fulfill God's plan for your life. Patience is the oven that God puts His children in, so we may cook at the right temperature and be fully mature at the right time.

Impatience is the microwave of the devil. It is synonymous with instant gratification; we short-circuit God's process; we want things instantly and not in God's time; we move not in God's time but in our own. It is designed to take everything of value out of your life and to take quality out of your productivity. Impatience

> **BE Thought of the Day**
>
> Patience is the oven that God puts his children in, so they may cook at the right temperature and be fully mature at the right time.

destroys marriages, friendships, businesses, and can even destroy your life.

Patience is doing what you can while waiting on God to do what only He can. Patience is God's plan to give you everything that you desire according to His timing, which is in line with His plan for your life. Patience is produced through trials, and we need patience to have character, for without character we have no hope. Hope is essential to realizing our business and personal goals and objectives. (Romans 5:3-4)

Allowing patience to be complete in us allows us to be complete on the inside and out; lacking nothing. God wants us to be whole. He wants us to completely depend on Him and Him only. He wants us to have life and have it more abundantly. The only way for Him to help us achieve complete internal wholeness and walk in abundant life is to allow us to persevere. Continue to be patient because God is taking you somewhere and the greater the suffering the greater the reward; the greater the sacrifice, the greater the fruit.

BE Prayer of the Day

Father, forgive me for being impatient and not waiting on Your perfect time. I ask for the grace to overcome impatience while You take the time to develop my character, in Jesus' name, Amen.

BE Application of the Day

- What trials are you experiencing that are trying your patience?
- Choose to believe that God is using these trials for your good and begin to cultivate an attitude of patience.

_____
_____
_____
_____
_____
_____
_____
_____
_____
_____
_____
_____

- Reflect on these passages of scripture and explain how they relate to today's devotional: Hebrews 10:35-36 and James 5:10-11.

_____
_____
_____
_____
_____
_____
_____
_____
_____
_____
_____
_____
_____
_____

Day 12

WHAT IF CHRIST DID NOT RISE?

If there is no resurrection of the dead, then not even Christ has been raised. And if Christ has not been raised, our preaching is useless and so is your faith.

I Corinthians 15:13-14

Easter is the time of year when we celebrate the resurrection of our Lord and Savior Jesus Christ. For the Biblical Entrepreneur, it should be a time of reflection on the gift of salvation and the power of Christ's resurrection. As the Apostle Paul states in Philippians 3:10-11, *"I want to know Christ and the power of his resurrection and the fellowship of sharing in his sufferings, becoming like him in his death, and so, somehow, to attain to the resurrection from the dead."* What if He did not rise from the dead? If Christ did not rise from the dead, the consequences for us are great. If Christ did not rise, then our preaching is empty – meaning that there is no power in the Word of God, there is no salvation, there is no forgiveness of sins, and there is no need for a marketplace ministry or biblical entrepreneurship. We can therefore do business like the pagans since there would be no need to use our businesses as a tool to fulfill the Great Commission. Secondly, if Christ did not rise, our faith is empty – there is nothing for us to believe in, there would be no substance to our faith. We can only have confidence in what we can see and touch. Thirdly, if Christ did not rise, we are false witnesses – if this were so then all Christians, including Biblical Entrepreneurs, are liars since we are preaching about something that never happened. Everything that we believe would then be based on a lie. If Christ did not rise, then all those who claim to be Christians are fools; we are stupid and Biblical Entrepreneurship is based on a lie because the Bible would then be a book of lies. Thank God none of this is true, since Christ did rise from the dead. Because He rose from the dead, we are saved from death. Since Christ rose from the dead, the same power that raised

> ❧ BE Thought of the Day
>
> Since Christ rose from the dead, the same power that raised Him from death can help us overcome any dead situation in our lives and businesses.

Him from death can help us overcome any dead situation in our lives and businesses. Since Christ rose from the dead, our faith is based on truth and can therefore move mountains. Since Christ rose from the dead, we are in right standing with God and are true witnesses of the resurrection. Since Christ rose, we have hope in this life and in the life to come. Since all of this is true, we can do business God's way; we can use our businesses as tools to fulfill the Great Commission and be His ambassadors in the marketplace. Thank God that He has risen. He is risen indeed!

BE Prayer of the Day
Father, I thank You that my faith is based on a resurrected Savior. I pray that my life and business will be filled with the power of Christ's resurrection, in Jesus' name, Amen.

BE Application of the Day

- Are there any areas of your life or business that are dead?
- Begin to believe that God is willing and able to resurrect all dead areas of your life.

_____
_____
_____
_____
_____
_____
_____
_____
_____
_____
_____
_____
_____
_____

- Reflect on these passages of scripture and explain how they relate to today's devotional: Luke 24:13-35 and Romans 8:11.

_____
_____
_____
_____
_____
_____
_____
_____
_____
_____
_____
_____
_____
_____

Day 13

THE FALL OF BABYLON

With a mighty voice he shouted: Fallen! Fallen is Babylon the Great! She has become a home for demons and a haunt for every evil spirit, a haunt for every unclean and detestable bird! **Revelation 18:2**

Babylon, an ancient city in the Old Testament, lies between the Tigris and Euphrates rivers. It served as the capital of the Babylonian Empire and is one of the oldest cities in the ancient world. Babylon was founded by Nimrod the Great who attempted to lead people into building a tower that would reach the heavens. This was an act of pride and rebellion against God. As a result, God confounded their language. Babylon was known for its worship of false gods, its power, wealth, extravagance, and cruelty. It destroyed Jerusalem and deported the citizens of Judah. Jeremiah predicted its downfall. Eventually, Babylon fell. The book of Revelation uses the term "Babylon" as a symbol of a nation that has turned its back on God and turned the nations of the world with it. An angel in Revelation states, *"Fallen! Fallen is Babylon the Great, which made all the nations drink the maddening wine of her adulteries." (Rev 14:8)… "For all the nations have drunk the maddening wine of her adulteries. The kings of the earth committed adultery with her, and the merchants of the earth grew rich from her excessive luxuries" (Rev 18:3).* This nation has raised many kings of the earth into prominence. It has made many business men and women rich and wealthy while promoting a way of life that is full of excess. It has rejected God and promoted lifestyles, products and services that do not glorify God and are inconsistent with the Word of God. This nation is predicted to suffer under the wrath of God because of its defiance and its rebellion against our Lord and Savior Jesus Christ. When she falls, those who have benefited from her will stand at a distance because they will not want to go down with her. They will cry because they stand to lose

> ✍ BE Thought of the Day
>
> Biblical Entrepreneurs must be discerning as they operate in the world but not of the world, so that they do not fall prey to the lust and greed of this Babylonian spirit.

a great deal by her downfall. They will be shocked because in an hour its great riches will come to nothing. Biblical Entrepreneurs must be discerning as they operate in the world but not of the world, so that they do not fall prey to the lust and greed of this Babylonian spirit. We must be salt and light in the world rather than blending into the system; otherwise we will suffer the consequences of its downfall. We cannot be so determined to build our businesses that we buy into the Babylonian ways, because they lead to death and destruction. If we are so profit-driven that we compromise our values, we will lose our souls in the end. Our principle must be this: "It is better that I have a little and be right with my God, than to have a whole lot and not be right with my God. Pleasing Jesus is the most important thing in my life." Everything else must be subject to that purpose.

BE Prayer of the Day

Father, I pray that You will help me to be fully committed to You in every area of my life and business. Help me to not compromise my relationship with You for anything that this world has to offer, in Jesus' name, Amen.

BE Application of the Day

- Are you operating your business in Babylon? Can you discern between the Babylonian ways and the ways of God?
- Are you compromising your values in any areas of your business or lifestyle?
- Evaluate your life and make sure that pleasing God is the most important thing in your life.

_____

_____

_____

_____

_____

_____

_____

_____

_____

_____

_____

- Reflect on these passages of scripture and explain how they relate to today's devotional: Psalm 37 and Matthew 5:13-16.

_____

_____

_____

_____

_____

_____

_____

_____

_____

_____

_____

_____

_____

Day 14

MORE THAN A CONQUEROR

...in all these things we are more than conquerors through Him who loved us. **Romans 8:37**

If there is one thing that entrepreneurs need on a daily basis in order to cope with the pressures of business and the uncertainties of the marketplace, it is an internal sense of confidence in God. There are days when expenses exceed revenue and we do not know how to pay the rest of our bills. There are days we get disappointing news from a client, a vendor, or an employee that causes us to wonder whether or not we will be able to remain in business. No matter what the challenge, the good news is that we can always turn to the Word of God and find comfort and encouragement.

Romans 8:35 tells us that nothing shall separate us from the love of God in Christ Jesus; not tribulation (a condition of affliction), distress (a state of adversity), persecution (persistent mistreatment), famine (severe lack of natural provision), nakedness (being without natural protection), peril (potential cause of loss) or sword (weapons used against us) (KJV). Verse 37 further states, *"... in all these things we are more than conquerors through him who loved us."* This means that in times of tribulation, distress, persecution, famine, nakedness, peril, or sword we are victorious. To be more than a conqueror means to have overwhelming and exceeding victory over the enemy or a situation. Whatever situation you are facing, whatever your circumstances are, you have overwhelming and exceeding victory.

> ✺ BE Thought of the Day
>
> Whatever situation you are facing, whatever your circumstances are, you have overwhelming and exceeding victory.

While I was in my senior year of high school, I was the captain of my basketball team. I thought I was pretty good, but let's suppose I was to challenge Michael Jordan in a one-on-one contest. Would I have a chance to win the game?

No, he would have overwhelmingly defeated me. Not only would I not win the game, but I would have no chance of winning. Michael Jordan is a superior basketball player compared to me. That is the same way with you and whatever situation you are facing. You have superiority over your situation not because of you, but because of Christ who loves you.

The question becomes not whether we have this superiority over the enemy and our situation, because we do. Rather the question becomes why do believers allow themselves to be overcome by the enemy? The simple answer is that we do not walk in the victory we have and we give place to the enemy. Being more than a conqueror is not situational; it is a state of being. You conquered before you even started; your victory is not based on what you do but on what Christ did on the Cross of Calvary. All you have to do is walk in your victory and do not give place to the enemy. Let me use another personal example, I struggle with timeliness and the Lord has assured me that I am more than a conqueror in the area of timeliness. However I have not been walking in that victory and I give place to the enemy by not giving myself enough time to get to where I need to go. I often abuse the grace of God by giving myself just enough time without considering that things could go wrong. Walking in my victory means I must plan to be early so I will not be late. I must also give myself more than enough time so that no matter what the enemy attempts to do, it will not affect my timeliness because the advantage is on my side.

Regardless of the issues that you may be struggling with, may our Lord Jesus Christ give you the grace to achieve overwhelming and exceeding victory in your business and in all areas of your life for His glory.

BE Prayer of the Day

Father, I thank You that You have made me more than a conqueror in Christ Jesus. I pray that You enable me to have Christ's victory in every area of my business, in Jesus' name, Amen.

BE Application of the Day

- What issues are you struggling with? Are you walking in your victory? Are you giving place to the devil? Remember the advantage is on your side.
- Identify the various obstacles you need to overcome and begin to thank God that you have overcome them.
- Pray for the wisdom to discern the areas where you may be giving place to the devil so that you can resist him and give him no place.

_____

_____

_____

_____

_____

_____

_____

_____

_____

_____

_____

- Reflect on these passages of scripture and explain how they relate to today's devotional: Jeremiah 1:19 and John 16:33.

_____

_____

_____

_____

_____

_____

_____

_____

_____

_____

_____

_____

_____

Day 15

7 STEPS TO FINANCIAL VICTORY

She went and told the man of God, and he said, "Go, sell the oil and pay your debts. You and your sons can live on what is left." **2 Kings 4:7**

In 2 Kings 4:7, a widow is facing bankruptcy and a creditor is about to take her children to be his slave. Led by the Spirit of God, she goes to the prophet Elisha to get some help. Elisha does not give this widow any money but gives her 7 ways to use her assets to become financially free:

1. **Assess your current assets** – Elisha asked the widow to assess her current assets, but her response demonstrated that she did not value what she had. She felt she had nothing but a jar of oil (2 Kings 4:2). Many of us suffer because we undervalue what God has placed in our hands. God used that jar of oil to set her financially free. What do you have in your hands?

2. **Borrow to produce and not consume** – You should never borrow to consume, only to produce. Elisha instructed the widow to borrow in 2 Kings 4:3. We must be careful to borrow enough to take us out of debt versus borrowing to place us in more debt. God instructed the Israelites not to lend money to each other because it was never His plan that we should live from debts. You only borrow to invest in a business or a project that will generate enough returns to pay back the debt and allow you to make a profit. Should you lack basic necessities, (food, clothing and shelter) ask God to show you how to use your assets to generate the money or for someone to show you kindness by sowing into your life instead of you borrowing to survive.

3. **Block out all distractions** – Many times we do not accomplish our objectives because of the many distractions in our lives. Elisha instructed the widow to go into her house and shut the door behind her so she would not be distracted by anyone or anything (2 Kings 4:3). What is distracting you? Ask God for the courage to reject it and seek first the Kingdom.

> ℰ BE Thought of the Day
>
> God never leaves any of His children without an asset.

4. **Get the help of others, especially your family** – Sometimes pride keeps us from asking others for help and of course we know what the Bible says about pride; it comes before a fall. Other times we do not want others to experience the struggle so we shield them. This does not allow them to learn and grow from the experience. Elisha instructed the widow to enlist the children in the business (2 Kings 4:3). Who can you enlist to help you achieve your goals at this time?

5. **Trust God for supernatural assistance** – Just because you are a Christian and you have a need, does not mean that God will intervene supernaturally. Once you have obeyed God's principles and maximized your abilities, God supernaturally comes in to assist according to your faith. Of course there are times that even in our disobedience, God supernaturally comes in as an act of mercy but we should not plan around that because He said He will have mercy on whom He chooses to have mercy. God multiplied the oil to fill every vessel that the widow borrowed. The oil increased in proportion to her faith, which was demonstrated by the number of vessels she borrowed (2 Kings 4:5-6).

6. **Sell for profit** – Unfortunately, many people look down on selling or are afraid to sell because of how they believe others will view them. Selling is not bad. Selling is an opportunity to provide something of value to someone who needs it in exchange for something of value. Elisha instructed the widow to go to the marketplace and sell her oil for profit (2 Kings 4:7). What product or service do you have that you can sell for a profit?

7. **Pay your debts and live on the rest** – The key to achieving our financial victory is repaying those who we borrowed from and having enough left to take care of our family. Elisha instructed the widow to pay her debt and live on the rest with her sons (2 Kings 4:7). Who must you repay who invested in you during your time of need?

BE Prayer of the Day

Father, I ask You to help me access the assets You have given me. I pray that You will also grant me the wisdom I need to utilize those assets in order to achieve victory in my finances, in Jesus' name, Amen.

BE Application of the Day

- What asset has God placed in your hand?
- Are you on your way to financial victory?
- If not, apply these steps and through God's wisdom begin to walk in your victory.

_____

_____

_____

_____

_____

_____

_____

_____

_____

_____

_____

_____

_____

- Reflect on these passages of scripture and explain how they relate to today's devotional: Proverbs 27:23 and Ecclesiastes 11:1-6.

_____

_____

_____

_____

_____

_____

_____

_____

_____

_____

_____

_____

_____

Day 16

GOD'S GRACE IS SUFFICIENT

...My grace is sufficient for you, for my power is made perfect in weakness.

2 Corinthians 12:9

Some people believe that being victorious in Christ means living a trouble-free life. This is a lie from the enemy and an attempt to keep God's servants distracted from serving, and distracted by what the Apostle Paul called light afflictions. I have witnessed many biblical entrepreneurs, and others who aspire to be witnesses for God in the marketplace, face various types of problems. You would think that since you are committed to serving God with all your heart, mind, and strength, that He would protect you from trouble. After all isn't it to God's advantage that we succeed? This may be true and God does want us to succeed, but we must be careful how we define success. With God, success means greater responsibility. However success is not devoid of problems. Through God's help, you can be successful in the midst of trouble, persecution, and distress. In God's economy, success and problems often go hand in hand. The Apostle Paul, one of the most successful apostles in the New Testament, achieved his success in spite of the troubles he faced. There was a particular problem that he faced throughout his ministry that seemed unbearable to him. He prayed to God three times about this problem and God's response to him was *"...My grace is sufficient for you, for my power is made perfect in weakness..."* (I Corinthians 12:9). With this response from God, the Apostle Paul's decision was, *"...Therefore I will boast all the more gladly about my weaknesses, so that Christ's power may rest on me. That is why, for Christ's sake, I delight in weaknesses, in insults, in hardships, in persecutions, in difficulties. For when I am weak, then I am strong."* (2 Corinthians 12:9 -10).

The grace of God is the undeserving favor and kindness of God that

> **BE Thought of the Day**
>
> The devil wants to use problems to distract you from fulfilling God's plan for your life and destroy God's purpose for you, but God wants to use the same problems to perfect and humble you.

works on our behalf. This grace operates based on His covenantal will for our lives. No matter what problem you are facing, do not allow it to distract you. The devil wants to use problems to distract you from fulfilling God's plan for your life and destroy God's purpose for you, but God wants to use the same problems to perfect and humble you. Remember, the devil wants to steal, kill, and destroy your life, but Jesus wants to give you life and give it to you more abundantly. This abundant life can come in the midst of trouble and problems. Do not believe the lie that because you are a Christian you will have a trouble-free life. Rather, believe that because you are a Christian, you will have an abundant life in the midst of trouble as a result of God's sufficient grace. By sufficient, the Lord means His grace is enough. No matter what your trouble, there is always enough grace to see you through and His strength is made perfect in your weakness. God's strength is best experienced in your moments of weakness. When you cannot, God shows up; when you are limited, His unlimited power comes in; when it is no longer possible for you, He does the impossible; when you are weak, you are strong, because you are now able to tap into the strength of God.

One of my good friends, Art Ally of The Timothy Plan, often asks the question, "When are you closer to God? When you have plenty of money or when you have limited funds?" The response is always, "When we have limited funds." This is because when we have limited funds, we tend to pray more, we tend to be more sensitive to the Spirit of God, and we tend to be less distracted by other things. Choose to glorify God regardless of what you may be experiencing.

BE Prayer of the Day

Father, I thank You for the grace that is available to me in the midst of my toughest circumstances. I choose to praise You and trust that Your power will be made perfect in my weakness, according to Your Word, in Jesus' name, Amen.

BE Application of the Day

- What problems are you facing now?
- No matter what they are, gladly boast in them so that the power of Jesus may rest upon you.
- Take great pleasure in the problems you are currently facing for the sake of the Gospel. When you are weak, then you are strong, because God's omnipotent power is working in your favor.

_____
_____
_____
_____
_____
_____
_____
_____
_____
_____
_____
_____

- Reflect on these passages of scripture and explain how they relate to today's devotional: Psalm 34:1-10 and 1 Peter 1:1-7.

_____
_____
_____
_____
_____
_____
_____
_____
_____
_____
_____
_____
_____
_____

Day 17

FAR ABOVE RUBIES

Who can find a virtuous woman? For her price is far above rubies.

Proverbs 31:10 (KJV)

Mother's Day is a day set aside every year throughout the United States and some parts of the world to honor mothers and celebrate motherhood. I am personally grateful to my grandmother, my mother, my wife, my sisters, aunts and the many women who have positively impacted my life. Like the virtuous woman, their price is far above rubies. There are no successful entrepreneurs who can say that their grandmother, mother, or wife was not critical to their success. Women are the backbone of our society; they can cause us to fail or succeed. We cannot choose our grandmother or our mothers, but we can choose our wives. You can only be as successful as the person you marry. In Proverbs 31:10-31, the Bible mentions a woman, a virtuous woman, whose worth is far above rubies. A ruby is one of the great precious stones, usually more costly than a diamond of the same size. The Bible states that the worth of this woman is far above this great, precious stone. What would make a woman worth so much? Here are a few of her characteristics:

- **She is trustworthy** – Her husband does not have to worry about anything as far as she is concerned. He entrusts her with his finances, his deep inner fears and concerns, his children, even his business affairs.

- **She is industrious** – This woman is a biblical entrepreneur, she not only supports her husband, but takes every opportunity to use the talents that God has placed on the inside of her. She is never idle and is profitable in all of her endeavors.

> ✍ BE Thought of the Day
>
> Women are the backbone of our society; they can cause us to fail or succeed.

- **She is a homemaker** – Beyond being a business woman, she is also concerned about the things of her home. She realizes that her first responsibility is the stability of her home.
- **She is a wise steward** – She is a great manager of resources. She is not a consumer but a producer. She resists the temptation of spending money on things that have no eternal value. She generously gives to those in need.
- **She is gentle and wise in her speech** – She has a meek and quiet demeanor, but when she speaks, wisdom comes out of her mouth. She has hidden the Word of God in her heart, and out of the abundance of her heart she speaks.
- **She is a nurturing and caring mother** – She takes her responsibility as a mother very seriously. She does not allow anything to get in the way of providing nurturing care to her children to ensure their spiritual and natural success.
- **She fears the Lord** – She recognizes that her external beauty must be the result of an internal reverence for the Lord.

I know you may be wondering, "Does this woman really exist?" Yes she does. I married one. I believe every woman is born with the potential of being a virtuous woman. How fully developed she become depends on her upbringing and the influences she has in her life. It is the responsibility of the husband to provide the leadership and nurturing that will allow her to fully blossom to become the virtuous woman God has called her to be.

BE Prayer of the Day

Women's prayer
Lord, I know that my price is far above rubies, help me to become the virtuous woman that you have called me to be. In Jesus' name, Amen

Men's prayer
Lord, help me to nurture my wife or the women around me to realize their full potential in You, to Your glory and honor. In Jesus' name, Amen

BE Application of the Day

- What is your real opinion of your wife? Is she the virtuous woman you desire her to be? Seek God for wisdom on how to support her in becoming all that she can be.
- If you are a woman and believe you do not reflect the characteristics above, seek God for wisdom on how to cultivate those characteristics for His glory.

_____

_____

_____

_____

_____

_____

_____

_____

_____

_____

_____

_____

- Reflect on these passages of scripture and explain how they relate to today's devotional: Genesis 2:20-24 and 1 Peter 3:1-6.

_____

_____

_____

_____

_____

_____

_____

_____

_____

_____

_____

_____

_____

Day 18

JOSEPH, A JUST MAN

Then Joseph her husband, being a just man, and not willing to make her a public example, was minded to put her away privily. **Matthew 1:19 (KJV)**

A father is not only a man, but also a husband, a dad, a son, and a brother. He must demonstrate total faithfulness in all his relationships. Let us look to the scriptures to identify a man we can learn from. The Bible does not say a lot about this man, but the little that is said about him gives us a clear indication of the type of person he was. Just imagine that you are God and you devise a plan to save humanity from destruction and eternal punishment. Your plan involves impregnating an engaged woman who will raise the Savior of the world with her husband. The problem is you have to do it within an environment and culture where there are certain religious laws and customs that can hinder your plans. For instance, the woman you choose to impregnate can be put to death for having committed adultery if her husband does not cooperate; her husband may not take responsibility to be the father of a child who is not his biologically. Your plans cannot work unless you find a woman who is engaged to be married to a just man. Just means: Righteous, Precise, Balanced. A just man is one who is right with God and seeks to live his life in accordance with the Word of God by the leading of His Spirit. The man the Lord found was Joseph, the son of Jacob, from the lineage of King David. Joseph was a young businessman from Nazareth, who operated a carpentry business. He was engaged to Mary, a young virgin and was looking forward to getting married. However, Joseph's world is turned upside down when he is informed by Mary that she is pregnant. Knowing that he is not the father, Joseph begins to make plans to cancel the engagement. As Joseph contemplates how to deal with the situation, he gets a visit from an angel of God, through a

> **BE Thought of the Day**
>
> Joseph lived a life that reflected complete obedience to the scriptures. He was a Just man.

69

dream, to inform him that the child his wife is carrying is of the Holy Spirit. In other words, God Himself is the father of his child and the child's name is Jesus who came to seek and save the lost. Wow! How would you handle this type of news? What was it about Joseph that God could trust him with such an assignment? What made Joseph such a <u>Just Man</u>?

- He was righteous – Joseph lived a life that reflected complete obedience to the scriptures. He was a Just man. **Matthew 1:19**
- He was gracious – Though Joseph thought that Mary potentially had sinned against God, he was careful not to do anything to embarrass her or hurt her. He planned to put her away secretly. He exemplified the scripture that says love covers a multitude of sins. **Matthew 1:19**
- He was sensitive to God's Spirit – As he contemplated how to handle the situation, he left himself open for the Spirit of God to speak to him. **Matthew 1:20-21**
- He was obedient – When God spoke to him, he did not hesitate to act on God's instructions. **Matthew 1:24**
- He was disciplined – Most of us look forward to getting married so we can enjoy our new bride sexually. Joseph demonstrated great discipline by keeping himself from his bride until she gave birth to the baby Jesus. **Matthew 1:25**
- He was a protector – Once he recognized, through the warnings of God's angels that the child Jesus was in danger, he moved quickly to protect him and his new wife by traveling to another country. **Matthew 2:13-15**
- He was a provider – Joseph was a businessman. He provided for his family through his carpentry business. **Mark 6:3**

BE Prayer of the Day

Father, help me to live a life completely yielded to You and to be a just person, as Joseph was, in Jesus' name, Amen.

BE Application of the Day

- What type of father are you?
- Can the Lord trust you with an assignment that will impact eternity?
- Reflect on the characteristics that made Joseph just, and seek the Lord as to how you can enhance your own character to reflect those attributes.
- If you are a woman, seek the Lord for how you can help your husband develop those attributes.

_____
_____
_____
_____
_____
_____
_____
_____
_____
_____
_____

- Reflect on these passages of scripture and explain how they relate to today's devotional: Genesis 6: 8-9 and Psalm 1.

_____
_____
_____
_____
_____
_____
_____
_____
_____
_____
_____
_____

Day 19

WE EACH HAVE A RESPONSIBILITY TO TRADE OUR ASSETS

Then he that had received the five talents went and traded with the same, and made them other five talents. And likewise he that had received two, he also gained other two.

Matthew 25:16-17 (KJV)

The value of our assets cannot increase unless we trade them. An asset not put to use loses its value over time. To trade is to exchange something of value with an expectation of a higher return; it is to do business or to be productive. "Business is God's idea but success is our responsibility" is a theme often quoted in Biblical Entrepreneurship. What we mean by this statement is that man did not come up with the idea of business, God did. It was God who after creating man, instructed him to be fruitful and multiply, fill the earth and subdue it, and have dominion. It was God who after establishing the Garden of Eden gave man the instructions to dress it and to keep it or to care for it. It was God who after giving the talents to the servant, said "occupy or do business until I come". Each of these instructions was talking about business or productivity. Though God's original plan did not include commerce as we know it today, business was a central part of it. Commerce came as a result of the consequences of sin (Gen 2:16, Gen 3:17 -19). God has done His part by giving us the assets and the instructions, now it is our responsibility to obey them and be faithful over that which we have stewardship, so we may be able to give an account. **Stewardship** is caring for the things (assets) of another. Whether you start a business or not, God requires you to be productive with the assets He gave you. To be productive means to work in such a manner that you can yield a profit. Some of us just work, never asking ourselves if our labor is yielding a profit. The question is not just about getting paid for what you do, but rather it is about creating value

> ✍ BE Thought of the Day
>
> God has done His part by giving us the assets and the instructions, now it is our responsibility to obey the instructions, thus ensuring our success.

through your work. All of us will not start a business but all of us are stewards; therefore, whether we are business stewards or a steward who is employed by someone else, we each must render an account before God for our productivity. You do not start a business to make money, but through business, money is generated. Some of the money generated is called a profit. That profit is the tangible demonstration of your stewardship. It is the fruit of good stewardship. You are always expected by God to appreciate the value of whatever He puts under your hands. The objective of a steward is to appreciate the value of things for which he is responsible. If you buy a car, your stewardship of that car, or how well you take care of that car, will be demonstrated by the resale value of the car. Though cars tend to depreciate in value, if you take good care of them, they will not depreciate as much, and you will have a better resale value. With this in mind, when you trade the assets which God has entrusted to you, God expects you to appreciate them or to multiply them through your stewardship.

BE Prayer of the Day

Father, thank You for all the assets You have given me. Please help me to be faithful with them and to put them to use so that they may increase in value, in Jesus' name, Amen.

BE Application of the Day

- Are you obeying God's instructions concerning the assets He has given you?
- Are you being faithful with those assets whether they are your own or someone else's?
- Examine your work. Is your work yielding a profit?
- Are you increasing the value of your assets through your stewardship?

_____
_____
_____
_____
_____
_____
_____
_____
_____
_____
_____

- Reflect on these passages of scripture and explain how they relate to today's devotional: II Kings 4:1-7 and Proverbs 14:23.

_____
_____
_____
_____
_____
_____
_____
_____
_____
_____
_____
_____
_____
_____

Day 20

GET BEHIND ME SATAN

Jesus turned and said to Peter, "Get behind me, Satan! You are a stumbling block to me; you do not have in mind the things of God, but the things of men."

Matthew 16:23

"You can't do it", "you won't succeed" or "you are not ready." These are words that entrepreneurs hear often from their loved ones, their friends, and even those who are co-laboring with them. Like Jesus, we must be bold enough to say, when appropriate, "Get behind me Satan!" These harsh words were spoken by Jesus Christ to one of His disciples, His closest companion, the one He would put in charge of providing leadership for the new organization He was about to establish. They were spoken right after Peter had just been used by God to reveal that Jesus was the Christ, the Son of the living God. That is interesting. One minute God is using Peter to speak one of the greatest revelations in the New Testament – who Christ is. The next minute Jesus Christ Himself is accusing Peter of being an agent of Satan who is not mindful of the things of God, but of the things of men. Jesus had just finished telling His disciples the plans of His death and resurrection when Peter pulled Him aside and began to rebuke Him, saying that it would not happen.

As a leader, Jesus had the ability to discern when His disciples were being used by God versus when the enemy was using them. He understood that if the enemy could not cause Him to sin directly, he would use someone close to Him. As leaders and Biblical Entrepreneurs, we must learn a lesson from the Master. If the devil cannot cause us to abandon the mission, he may use someone really close to us to distract us from the mission. Often times, he uses those whom we trust the most, even our family members. Those he uses are often not aware that they are being used

> ✍ BE Thought of the Day
>
> If the devil cannot cause us to abandon the mission, he may use someone really close to us to distract us from the mission.

by the devil, since they are not conscious of their own motivation. Peter's motivation was to protect Jesus from suffering and death, but what he missed was that suffering and death were the roadways to Jesus realizing His mission. In trying to protect Jesus, he was committing the sin of self-preservation. The sin of self-preservation occurs when we are more concerned with protecting our earthly interest than securing our heavenly reward. We commit this sin when we become so earthly-minded that we are no heavenly good, or when as ambassadors we forget that we are but pilgrims passing through and the earth is not our home. We are here on a heavenly assignment. You must clearly know the road map to fulfilling your mission since all roads will not take you there. Thus, you have to have a plan. It is therefore your responsibility to communicate that plan to your team and those whom the Lord has called to co-labor with you. Communicating the plan to your team does not guarantee that they will follow or even support the plan since they have a free will. You must discern who is not following and supporting the plan in the name of self-preservation. As a leader, as a Biblical Entrepreneur, as a husband or wife, and as a parent, you must be bold enough to say to those you love and trust, "Get behind me Satan". These are the moments when you discern that the enemy is using them to distract you from the mission. Ultimately, God will hold you responsible and not them.

BE Prayer of the Day

Father, I pray that You would help me to be like Christ and not allow anyone to keep me from fulfilling Your purpose for my life. Help me to discern when the enemy is using others to distract me, and give me the grace to not commit the sin of self-preservation, in Jesus' name, Amen.

BE Application of the Day

- Are you allowing anyone to deter you from fulfilling your mission? Be bold enough to say, "Get behind me Satan!"
- Are you committing the sin of self-preservation? Like Christ, choose to focus on your heavenly reward regardless of the road you may have to travel.

_____

_____

_____

_____

_____

_____

_____

_____

_____

_____

_____

_____

- Reflect on these passages of scripture and explain how they relate to today's devotional: Genesis 3:17 and 1 Samuel 17:28.

_____

_____

_____

_____

_____

_____

_____

_____

_____

_____

_____

_____

Day 21

PROFIT IS THE FRUIT OF PROPER STEWARDSHIP, NOT THE REWARD

The man who had received the five talents brought the other five. "Master," he said, "you entrusted me with five talents. See, I have gained five more" … The man with the two talents also came. "Master," he said, "you entrusted me with two talents; see, I have gained two more."
Matthew 25:20, 22

Most business schools and consultants believe and teach that the goal of the entrepreneur is to make a profit and increase his standard of living; this is the reward of being a good entrepreneur. In Biblical Entrepreneurship, the business profit is not your reward for being a good entrepreneur or a good steward. Remember the assets that you start the business with are not yours. The gifts, skills, and treasures are not yours; they are the Master's who has entrusted them to your care until He returns. For example, suppose you are a money manager and I give you $25,000 to care for. Ten years later, I return to you for my investment. Based on your good stewardship, you increased it from $25,000 to $200,000. How much money do you owe me $25,000 or $200,000? Of course the answer will be $200,000, because the $25,000 you began with was not yours and neither is the increase of $175,000. The assets you began with belong to your Master and the increase of the assets is His as well; nothing belongs to you. So what does one do with the profit? The profit is used for the following three things:

1. To reinvest in the business – Many entrepreneurs get so focused on enhancing their standard of living that they miss the fact that you must continuously reinvest in the business in order to increase the capacity of that business to produce, thereby serving more people. This should be the goal of every business.

2. **Enhance your products and services** – The sad reality is that many entrepreneurs begin with great products and services, but instead of improving those products and services over time, they look for ways to cut costs in order to make more money. Don't get me wrong, you should always be on the lookout for more affordable ways to produce and deliver your goods, but never at the expense of quality. I am sure you can think of many products or services that have decreased in quality over time.

3. **To fulfill God's covenant** – Deuteronomy 8:18 tells us that God has given us power so that we may gain wealth to fulfill His covenant. It is no coincidence that right after the parable of the talents, the Lord Jesus Christ tells us the story of how He will judge the nations in Matthew 25:31–46. According to this story, the business profit is to be used to feed the hungry, nourish the thirsty, house the stranger, clothe the naked, and visit the sick and those who are in prison. I believe that these key areas of focus have both spiritual and natural implications.

Make sure that your business profits are being used in such a manner that the Master can be pleased.

BE Prayer of the Day

Father, thank You for the profits that my stewardship is generating, I pray for direction to know how to use those profits so that I may further glorify You, in Jesus' name, Amen.

BE Application of the Day

- How are you using your business profits?
- In what ways can you reinvest in your business?
- In what ways can you increase the quality of your product or service?
- In what ways can you use your profit to fulfill God's covenant?

_____

_____

_____

_____

_____

_____

_____

_____

_____

_____

_____

_____

- Reflect on these passages of scripture and explain how they relate to today's devotional: Deuteronomy 10:12-14 and Hebrews 13:1-3.

_____

_____

_____

_____

_____

_____

_____

_____

_____

_____

_____

_____

_____

Day 22

7 BUSINESS LESSONS FROM THE MASTER

After a long time the master of those servants returned and settled accounts with them.

Matthew 25:19

In Matthew 25, there are important lessons that the master of the servants, who represents our Lord Jesus Christ, can teach us, based on how he managed his servants. Usually, we tend to focus on how the servants handled their talents. The real businessman in this story is the master. What business lessons can we learn from him?

1. **He had some assets to invest** – The master gave his servants his assets to invest; he made sure they did not remain idle while he was traveling (Matthew 25:14). An asset is something you have of value that can generate revenue. Make sure that you are always aware of your assets and how to put them to work. Revenue generation begins with proper asset allocation.

2. **He prepared his servants** – He gave them talents according to their abilities (Matthew 25:15-16). He made sure that his servants were equipped to handle the talents he gave them. He did not give them more than they could handle but what he knew they could manage. We must ensure that our staff members are properly trained and equipped to do what we expect of them.

3. **He diversified his investments** – The master put his investments in the hands of his most trusted servants. He could have given all the investments to the servant who was able to multiply them the most, but that would have increased his risk of entrusting all of his eggs to only one basket. Thus, he diversified them. Diversifying ensures that you minimize your risks, maximize your returns, and protect your assets against possible loss.

> **⁊᷿ BE Thought of the Day**
>
> It is our responsibility to apply these principles in our business affairs; otherwise we will suffer the consequence of being disciplined by our Master, the Lord Jesus Christ.

4. **He delegated responsibility** – After he gave them the talents, he went on a journey (Matthew 25:15). He left them to take full responsibility for their assignments. We must not micro-manage our staff members, but rather, we must demonstrate our trust in their abilities by allowing them to handle their responsibilities.
5. **He held them accountable** – After a long time the master returned and settled accounts with them (Matthew 25:19). Although he trusted their ability, he kept them accountable. A lack of accountability produces a lack of performance and even hurts morale.
6. **He rewarded them for their productivity** – Individuals are driven by incentives. Hopefully you have a strategic plan with clear measurable goals and objectives. Tie those goals to a reward system to teach your team that productivity will be rewarded. Do not reward people for what they should be doing already, and do not delegate their rewards to eternity, they need them now.
7. **He disciplined the unproductive servant** – The master rebuked the unproductive servant and gave his talent to the one with the 10 talents (Matthew 25:26-28). He confronted the unproductive servant, explained his disappointment, told him what he should have done, and administered the appropriate discipline. In the name of Christian love, some Christian owners or managers tend to create an undisciplined workplace. Remember, God chastises those He loves (Hebrews 12:6). If you do not have the courage to discipline your staff, you either do not love them or you are operating out of fear, which is not of God. Perfect love drives out fear (1 John 4:18).

It is our responsibility to apply these principles in our business affairs; otherwise we will suffer the consequence of being disciplined by our Master, the Lord Jesus Christ. That discipline may manifest itself in business failure and perhaps eventually in eternal punishment, as it did with the servant who had the one talent.

BE Prayer of the Day

Father, I ask You for the grace to apply these principles to my business affairs, following the example of my Master, Jesus Christ, in Jesus' name, Amen.

BE Application of the Day

- Examine the way you handle your business affairs.
- How can you apply these principles to the way you do business?

_____
_____
_____
_____
_____
_____
_____
_____
_____
_____
_____
_____
_____
_____

- Reflect on these passages of scripture and explain how they relate to today's devotional: Exodus 35:30-35 and Numbers 11:16-17.

_____
_____
_____
_____
_____
_____
_____
_____
_____
_____
_____
_____
_____
_____

Day 23
THE FEAR OF FAILURE

Then the man who had received the one talent came. "Master," he said, "I knew that you are a hard man, harvesting where you have not sown and gathering where you have not scattered seed. So I was afraid and went out and hid your talent in the ground. See, here is what belongs to you." **Matthew 25:24-25**

Fear is anxiety caused by real or perceived danger which can hinder our ability to be productive. Many Christians who struggle with fear are familiar with the acts of God, but are ignorant of His ways. This fact is demonstrated in scripture with Moses and the children of Israel. The children of Israel knew the acts of God, and hid in their tents when God invited them to come closer. Moses, who knew His ways, went up to the mountain of God, had the opportunity to speak to God 'face to face' and came away with the Ten Commandments.

Those who know the ways of God tend to:
- Have reverence for God
- Trust in the Lord in all their ways
- Be risk takers
- Focus on others
- Be content
- Be fulfilled
- Walk by faith

Those who limit themselves to God's acts tend to:
- Fear
- Doubt
- Experience stress and anxiety
- Display ungratefulness
- Display greed and selfishness
- Play it safe
- Display laziness
- Walk by sight and not by faith
- Have Confidence in Self
- Manipulate

🔖 BE Thought of the Day

Many Christians who struggle with fear are familiar with the acts of God, but are ignorant of His ways.

Study the story of Moses and the children of Israel on their journey from Egypt to the Promised Land and you will discover the aforementioned characteristics in them. The defense that the servant with one talent gave was that based on his knowledge of the master, he was afraid of what he would do if he lost the talents. Had he really known the master, who represents God, he would have known that He is a God of mercy, justice, forgiveness and compassion who works all things together for our good because we love him and are called according to His purpose. Which God are you familiar with? Have you hesitated to use your talents because of the fear that if you lose them or make mistakes God will punish you? Look at Adam, David, Peter and many others in the Bible who made mistakes even after experiencing the goodness of God. Though they suffered the consequences of their actions, God forgave and restored them. Never allow fear to hinder you from utilizing your talents.

BE Prayer of the Day

Father, please help me to draw closer to You and to know You more so that I will have a steadfast confidence in You, in Jesus' name, Amen.

BE Application of the Day

- What kind of attributes do you notice in yourself?
- Is your knowledge of God based only on His acts or do you know His ways?
- Seek to mature in your knowledge of God so that you may know Him for who He is and not just for what He does.

_____
_____
_____
_____
_____
_____
_____
_____
_____
_____
_____
_____

- Reflect on these passages of scripture and explain how they relate to today's devotional: Micah 7:18-19 and 1 John 4:18.

_____
_____
_____
_____
_____
_____
_____
_____
_____
_____
_____
_____
_____

Day 24

GOD'S ECONOMY REWARDS PRODUCTIVITY

Take the talent from him and give it to the one who has the ten talents... And throw that worthless servant outside, into the darkness, where there will be weeping and gnashing of teeth.   **Matthew 25: 28, 30**

Many feel that the marketplace is unfair because it tends to favor the rich and exclude the poor. This is particularly noticeable when comparing minority communities with other communities, or the West with other parts of the world. We tend to blame this disparity on the seemingly unjust capitalist system. However, capitalism is not the sole instrument responsible for the disparity of wealth in the world. In some cases, the responsibility lies with the communities or countries and their lack of productivity. God moves resources from the control of those who are not productive to the control of those who are.

It is our responsibility to be productive and to cause the talents and abilities the Lord has given us to increase in value. What God has purposed for us to have and to manage can be lost when we exercise poor stewardship over it. God is so concerned about stewardship that He would rather see a nonbeliever being productive with His resources than to leave them in the hands of a believer who is not productive. God is not a wasteful God. As we see in the Parable of the Talents in Matthew 25, the master took the talent of the servant who only had one and gave it to him who already had ten. It would appear to me that the servant with one talent was not treated fairly. He didn't lose the talent. And did the servant with the ten talents really need anymore? It seems to me that he had enough. Most people, including Christians, would consider this to be unfair. In God's economy, however, fairness is not the issue. The issue is justice. Justice involves that which is in line with God's

> ℘ BE Thought of the Day
>
> God is so concerned about stewardship that He would rather see a nonbeliever being productive with His resources than to leave them in the hands of a believer who is not productive.

character, while fairness is that which takes into account human reasoning and influence.

In God's economy, the important thing is not the fair and equitable distribution of resources. The important thing is the fulfillment of His ultimate plan. Because the person with one talent would not do the job, God moved on to the one who would. As the saying goes, "nothing personal, it was merely business"…God's business.

No act of God is ever unfair or fair, but just. He cannot be unjust. It was not fair that one man, Jesus, would die for the sins of the entire world, but it was just.

BE Prayer of the Day

Father, I reverence You because You are not a wasteful God. Help me to take my responsibility to be productive seriously so that I do not lose what You have given me, in Jesus' name, Amen.

BE Application of the Day

- Have you been a poor steward over God's resources?
- Have you taken the talents He has given you for granted?
- Examine your stewardship and realize that if you are not faithful with God's resources, they may be taken from you.

_____

_____

_____

_____

_____

_____

_____

_____

_____

_____

_____

_____

_____

- Reflect on these passages of scripture and explain how they relate to today's devotional: Proverbs 10:4 and Matthew 5:45.

_____

_____

_____

_____

_____

_____

_____

_____

_____

_____

_____

_____

_____

Day 25

ATTITUDE VERSUS ALTITUDE

But now your kingdom will not endure; the LORD has sought out a man after his own heart and appointed him leader of his people, because you have not kept the LORD's command.   **I Samuel 13:14**

Attitude is the way you carry yourself or behave. It is based on the information you receive which passes through your value system. Our attitude must be based on our personal relationship with the Lord Jesus Christ. Our Christ-like attitude will determine our altitude. Attitude is displayed by the way you treat others, and altitude is your ability to be raised into a certain position. Altitude in business can be viewed as having the money needed to start your own business, having a great or unique idea, or having all of the necessary relationships and resources.

A good example of how altitude and attitude work is found in the Book of 1 Samuel, in the battle between King Saul and David. King Saul had everything: the kingdom of Israel, the army, the weapons and all of the resources of the kingdom. However, David, a shepherd and a servant of the king, only had his relationship with God, his friendship with the king's son Jonathan, and a few friends. King Saul received information that David's popularity could cause him and his children to lose the kingdom. Since he was no longer in fellowship with God, what was most important to him was keeping the kingdom for himself and his family. He began to rely upon himself rather than on God and made a decision to kill David in order to protect his kingdom. Saul planned this, knowing that God had a mighty purpose for David's life and that David had not wronged him. David, knowing that King Saul was planning to kill him, did not seek revenge, but sought the Lord for safety and protection. Even when he had opportunities to kill Saul, he chose not to because he believed it was more important to please God

&a BE Thought of the Day

Our Christ-like attitude will determine our altitude.

than to protect himself. King Saul had the altitude, but David had the attitude. In the end, King Saul killed himself and David became king of Israel.

BE Prayer of the Day

Father, I ask You to forgive me for having the wrong attitude about any aspect of my life. Help me to be concerned about the condition of my heart toward You more than any other thing in my life, in Jesus' name, Amen.

BE Application of the Day

- Do you value your skills, resources, and position more than your relationship with God?
- If so, seek the Lord that He may give you a Christ-like mindset concerning your current position so you may have the same heart that David had.

_____
_____
_____
_____
_____
_____
_____
_____
_____
_____
_____
_____

- Reflect on these passages of scripture and explain how they relate to today's devotional: Proverbs 16:18-19 and Proverbs 23:17-18.

_____
_____
_____
_____
_____
_____
_____
_____
_____
_____
_____
_____
_____
_____

Day 26

WHY CHRISTIAN BUSINESSES FAIL

– By T.W. Grigsby

But thou shalt remember the LORD thy God: for it is he that giveth thee power to get wealth, that he may establish his covenant which he sware unto thy fathers, as it is this day. **Deuteronomy 8:18 (KJV)**

In many cases, why is the quality of goods and services provided by Christian businesses worse than those provided by non-Christian businesses? Why are Christians not setting the standards for business throughout the world? I believe the answer is simply a lack of knowledge of biblical and business administrative principles and practices. Christian business owners tend to lean to their own understanding and follow the practices of worldly businesses, or "make it up" as they go along. Therefore, too many of our Christian businesses are struggling, if not failing, both spiritually and naturally. What poor witnesses for the Lord.

Early in my Christian walk, a Christian businessman said to me, "I don't believe you can operate a business by the Word of God." With my very limited knowledge of the scriptures, I did not believe that statement to be true, and I am now fully persuaded that it is not true. Deuteronomy 8:18 states, *"But thou shalt remember the LORD thy God: for it is he that giveth thee power to get wealth, that he may establish his covenant..."* (KJV). We must understand and appreciate the advantages we have as Christians because He gives us this power. Much of that power resides in our relationship with the Holy Spirit. We must understand how to access that power in order to prosper according to God's will for our lives.

> ✌ BE Thought of the Day
>
> We must understand and appreciate the advantages we have as Christians because He gives us this power ... We must understand how to access that power in order to prosper according to God's will for our lives.

Christian businesses need more than instructions in the traditional functions of business. They also need instructions in the principles of God as they apply these functions. Unfortunately, many Biblical Entrepreneurs have not been exposed to biblically-based teachings that provide them with the sufficient and practical knowledge of God's Word that is needed to make the connection between their businesses, all other aspects of their lives and the individual plan of God for their lives. Because of this, they do not have the requisite information to make godly decisions; thus, they operate in a self-imposed bondage. 2 Corinthians 5:18 and 20 states, *"All this is from God, who reconciled us to himself through Christ and gave us the ministry of reconciliation ... We are therefore Christ's ambassadors..."* Here the scriptures tell us that we are representatives of Christ in the earth and that He has given us the ministry to seek and save the lost. The question that arises is: how do I exercise my role as ambassador for Jesus Christ in the conduct of my business affairs?

Successful business people can have a significant impact upon the laws, policies, and procedures in their communities because their spheres of influence tend to be larger than most. Therefore, it is of great importance that Christian business people be the most credible witnesses possible. In such perilous times as we now live in, we want the world to seek us for answers to conditions and situations in our communities and around the world. We want non-believers to have what we have (salvation and a relationship with Jesus Christ). We want current and aspiring Christian business owners to have the knowledge they need to grow in their relationship with the Lord as their businesses grow and prosper.

BE Prayer of the Day

Father, help me to use the knowledge You placed in Your Word to operate my business, to receive the power I need to get wealth, and to impact lives in all my spheres of influence, in Jesus' name, Amen.

BE Application of the Day

- Are you operating your business based on the knowledge and power you receive from God and His Word?
- Are you impacting others in your spheres of influence?

_____
_____
_____
_____
_____
_____
_____
_____
_____
_____
_____
_____
_____

- Reflect on these passages of scripture and explain how they relate to today's devotional: Genesis 41:15 and Proverbs 10:22.

_____
_____
_____
_____
_____
_____
_____
_____
_____
_____
_____
_____
_____
_____

Day 27

THE DANGERS OF THE PROMISED LAND

Be careful that you do not forget the LORD your God, failing to observe his commands, his laws and his decrees that I am giving you this day. **Deuteronomy 8:11**

After spending 40 years in the wilderness, the children of Israel arrived in the Promised Land only to face the potential of forgetting the God who had led them out of Egypt. Joshua declared to them: *"But if serving the LORD seems undesirable to you, then choose for yourselves this day whom you will serve, whether the gods your forefathers served beyond the River, or the gods of the Amorites, in whose land you are living. But as for me and my household, we will serve the LORD"* (Joshua 24:15). David, the man after God's own heart, after overcoming Saul and becoming king of Israel, could not overcome the allure of absolute power. He committed adultery with the wife of Uriah the Hittite and killed Uriah to conceal his sin.

Nathan had to confront King David, *"Then Nathan said to David, "You are the man! This is what the LORD, the God of Israel, says: 'I anointed you king over Israel, and I delivered you from the hand of Saul. I gave your master's house to you, and your master's wives into your arms. I gave you the house of Israel and Judah. And if all this had been too little, I would have given you even more. Why did you despise the word of the LORD by doing what is evil in his eyes? You struck down Uriah the Hittite with the sword and took his wife to be your own. You killed him with the sword of the Ammonites. Now, therefore, the sword will never depart from your house, because you despised me and took the wife of Uriah the Hittite to be your own." (2 Samuel 12:7-10).* There is a danger in success. I call it the dangers of the Promised Land. There are three key dangers:

> ✿ BE Thought of the Day
>
> As Biblical Entrepreneurs we must know that our biggest enemy is not failure but rather it could be the very success that we are seeking.

1. **Relying on your resources** – There is no more manna so we must work for our

provision. We have a tendency to rely on what we have rather than relying on God. It becomes very difficult to know when it was God or our resources that brought us through.

2. **Following other gods** – Now that we have options we may begin to worship the things that God created instead of God. Some even turn to other types of beliefs.

3. **Forgetting the purpose of the promise** – The purpose of the Promised Land is to fulfill God's covenant and not to satisfy our own personal pleasure and comfort.

As Biblical Entrepreneurs we must know that our biggest enemy is not failure but rather it could be the very success that we are seeking.

BE Prayer of the Day

Father, help me not to forget You when I reach my "promised land." Give me the grace to be true to You in all seasons of my life, in Jesus' name, Amen.

BE Application of the Day

- Are you relying on your own resources to provide for you?
- Are you slowly wandering to other gods?
- Have you forgotten the reason why God delivered you out of Egypt and into the Promised Land?

_____
_____
_____
_____
_____
_____
_____
_____
_____
_____
_____
_____
_____

- Reflect on these passages of scripture and explain how they relate to today's devotional: Deuteronomy 8 and Proverbs 30: 7-9.

_____
_____
_____
_____
_____
_____
_____
_____
_____
_____
_____
_____
_____
_____

Day 28

VISION VERSUS IDEAS

Where there is no vision, the people perish: but he that keepeth the law, happy is he.

Proverbs 29:18 (KJV)

Successful entrepreneurs are those who have clear business ideas that meet legitimate consumer needs and a vision to manage and grow the business through the ups and downs of the economy. However, most start-ups and even growing businesses struggle with the distinction between business vision and ideas, and some even use these two terms interchangeably. I am a firm believer that there is a clear difference between vision and ideas. **Ideas** are thoughts that exist in the mind that can be developed into products and services and are used to meet market needs. Knowledge is required to develop them. Without ideas, a vision lacks the substance to be fully manifested. Entrepreneurs who are able to develop their business ideas properly have a good start in the marketplace. As important as ideas are for a business to start, the business has limited growth without a clear vision. **Visions** are clear revelations that lead individuals to realize their ideas or fulfill God's plan for their lives. Visions are used to inspire. They are acquired through a relationship with God and tend to evolve over time. The difference between the mom and pop business and the business that is able to grow beyond that stage is vision. The difference between the business where employees are unfulfilled and the leadership team seems to be out of focus, and the one where there is employee fulfillment and clear direction is vision. Vision is that which takes the ideas beyond the founders' dreams. Vision draws a big circle and invites every body to participate. Vision is the ability for us to see beyond the problems. You cannot realize a vision by yourself; you will need the help of others. An entrepreneur can have several business ideas, but he or she must have only one vision. The ideas must all feed that main vision.

> **BE Thought of the Day**
>
> **Ideas** are thoughts that exist in the mind that can be developed into products and services... **Visions** are clear revelations that lead individuals to realize their ideas or fulfill God's plan for their lives.

Anything that is not in line with the vision must be cut off. Though several ideas can feed one vision, you must not attempt to implement several ideas at the same time; that is a recipe for failure. Focus on one idea, nurture it and stabilize it. Then based on the lesson learned from that one idea and the foundation that you have established from it, you can launch the other ideas as long as they are fueling the same vision. These days everybody wants to develop multiple streams of income, so they have several ideas going at the same time. However, some of the ideas are not even related. Multiple streams of income are good; the virtuous woman had multiple streams of income. The problem is when you have multiple bad streams. If the main stream is not working well, no matter how much you multiply it, your circumstances will not improve, and they may even become worse. Success is not defined by the number of streams you have working but rather by the habits that you have developed. If you are able to develop one good stream that flows from a great vision, you can then multiply that stream. However, if you do not have a good stream, you have nothing to multiply. As you consider the ideas that God has given you, select one main idea that is in line with your ultimate vision and develop it to its fullness. Then use the success habits you used in developing that one idea to begin to develop other ideas, as long as they are all in line with the vision. Evaluate what you are doing now and be bold enough to cut off those streams that are unrelated to your vision, or those streams that are out of season.

BE Prayer of the Day

Father, help me to realize the vision that You have placed in my heart and give me the grace to use the ideas You have given me to develop that vision to its fullness, in Jesus' name, Amen.

BE Application of the Day

- Differentiate between your business ideas and your vision for your business.
- Do you have other streams that are not related to your vision? Be willing to cut them off.

_____

_____

_____

_____

_____

_____

_____

_____

_____

_____

_____

_____

_____

- Reflect on these passages of scripture and explain how they relate to today's devotional: Habakkuk 2: 2-3 and John 15:1-2.

_____

_____

_____

_____

_____

_____

_____

_____

_____

_____

_____

_____

_____

_____

Day 29
DEVELOPING YOUR IDEAS

"Before I formed you in the womb I knew you, before you were born I set you apart; I appointed you as a prophet to the nations." **Jeremiah 1:5**

Every born-again believer is born with a pre-ordained purpose from God. Most believers limit that purpose to their function within their local church. As a result, most Christians do not realize that their business ideas must line up with God's purpose and plan for their lives if they are truly to glorify God through their businesses. In developing your business idea there are seven things to consider:

1. **Your motivation** — What is your motivation for starting this business? Your motivation determines your drive and inspiration for establishing the business. Your motivation as a Biblical Entrepreneur must be love for God and others (John 3:16). Your business idea must be a tool that you use to express your love for God and show love to others. This motivation ensures that you are starting your business in an area that you are passionate about, to serve a market that you sincerely care for.

2. **Your purpose as a disciple of Jesus Christ** — Why did God create you? What is your raison d'etre? All disciples of Jesus Christ were created to conform to the image and likeness of Christ and to be witnesses for Him in the earth realm. Your business idea must be a tool that enables you to fulfill this purpose (Romans 8:29).

3. **Your gifts, skills, and abilities** — What are your talents/assets? Do they match your business idea? Your gifts, skills, and abilities are the tools that God has given you to realize your business idea.

> 𝕭 BE Thought of the Day
>
> …most Christians do not realize that their business ideas must line up with God's purpose and plan for their lives, if they are to truly glorify God through their businesses.

God would not have you start a business in an area where you have no gifts or skills. You also do not want to start or grow the business beyond your ability to manage it effectively (Matthew 25:14-15).

4. **Your calling** — Each of us has a unique assignment from God. It is different from purpose because calling addresses the specific assignment that is unique to an individual. We all have the same purpose but different callings. That is why you do not want just to copy someone else's idea. God has a unique idea just for you. In some cases you may have the same idea that someone else has, but the way God has called you to carry it out is unique to you because of your calling. In Biblical Entrepreneurship, we believe that business is a calling just as much as pastoring or any other activity that Christians are called to. Do you believe God has called you to be in business? How does your business idea line up with God's calling upon your life? (I Corinthians 7:17-24)

5. **Assess the needs** — A need is a lack or problem that requires a business or ministry solution. Business is about meeting needs. You must identify a need for which you have a burden. It must also have a great enough demand that it can sustain a business. Remember, not every need is yours to meet, and not every need can be met profitably. Make sure that the need you have selected can sustain a business. What need is your business idea meeting? How big is that need? Are there enough people who need that idea to support a business? (Acts 6:1-3)

6. **Develop products and/or services** — People buy products and services. What product or services can you develop or identify to meet the need you have selected? (2 Kings 4:3-4)

7. **Have a vision** — Can you develop a plan to carry out the idea? Vision is essential to cultivating and developing the full potential of an idea. Vision allows you to see the future and to design a strategy for how to get there (Proverbs 29:18).

BE Prayer of the Day

Father, I thank You that You created me with everything I need to fulfill my purpose. Help me to develop ideas in ways that line up with Your will and purpose for my life, in Jesus' name, Amen.

BE Application of the Day

- Whether you have a business idea or not, use these seven things to develop your idea or evaluate your current idea to ensure that it lines up with God's purpose and plan for your life.

_____
_____
_____
_____
_____
_____
_____
_____
_____
_____
_____
_____
_____
_____
_____
_____

- Reflect on these passages of scripture and explain how they relate to today's devotional: Isaiah 49:1 and 2 Peter 1:2-4.

_____
_____
_____
_____
_____
_____
_____
_____
_____
_____
_____
_____
_____
_____

Day 30

THE ORIGIN OF IDEAS

If any of you lacks wisdom, he should ask God, who gives generously to all without finding fault, and it will be given to him.   **James 1:5**

Every successful business began with a good idea. Ideas are thoughts that exist in the mind that can be developed into a product or service. They are intellectual properties and their value is determined by the market. Many who want to be entrepreneurs are always hungry for good ideas, and some even go as far as to copy others' ideas believing that it will bring them the same success that the other person is experiencing. They do not realize that it takes more than just having the idea to develop a successful business. It also involves believing in the idea and being willing to persevere through the trials and challenges of the development stages. If you are looking for a good business idea, you do not have to copy or emulate someone else's. Ideas originate from God, the Father of our Lord and Savior Jesus Christ, through the operation of the Holy Spirit. All you have to do is go to God in prayer and He will reveal ideas to you. So getting the idea is the easy part if you have a personal relationship with the God who is the originator of ideas. The hard part is turning the idea into a successful business. Successful ideas are acquired by faith. What is the difference between the entrepreneur who is able turn his idea into a profitable business and the one who gives up along the way or allows other things to distract him? The difference is not skill or money but belief. No matter how great the idea, if you do not believe in it enough to give it all you have and persevere through the difficult times, you will not succeed. Faith is believing enough in something to act on it. And even though you do not see the immediate reward, you know that in time your efforts will pay off. Faith is believing in your idea despite what others say, because your confidence is in your God and the insight He has given

> ✍ BE Thought of the Day
>
> ...it takes more than just having the idea to develop a successful business; it also involves believing in the idea and being willing to persevere through the trials and challenges of the development stages.

you concerning the idea. You may say, "Well what about those who do not believe in God and are able to develop successful businesses, how are they able to have faith?" They do, they have faith in what they know. They believe enough in what they know about their idea to be willing to stake everything for it. You must also remember that God causes rain to fall on the just and the unjust. The rain can be the ideas He gives them. The problem with their faith is that it is limited to what they can see, what they have experienced, and what they have been exposed to. Our faith goes beyond what we can see, experience, and what we have been exposed to. Our faith rests in our trust in God. Our faith depends on the life, death, and resurrection of our Lord and Savior Jesus Christ. Our faith is based on the Bible, which is the Word of God.

BE Prayer of the Day

Father, I ask that You give me a business idea based on Your will for my life and the faith, perseverance, and determination to bring it to fruition, in Jesus' name, Amen.

BE Application of the Day

- Do you have a business idea? Are you working on your idea? Are you persevering through hard times?
- Seek God today for wisdom and allow Him to reveal to you an idea that is based on His calling for your life. Have the faith to bring it to pass.

_____

_____

_____

_____

_____

_____

_____

_____

_____

_____

_____

_____

- Reflect on these passages of scripture and explain how they relate to today's devotional: Matthew 17:20-21 and James 1:17.

_____

_____

_____

_____

_____

_____

_____

_____

_____

_____

_____

_____

_____

Day 31

ENVY NOT THE OPPRESSOR

Envy thou not the oppressor, and choose none of his ways. **Proverbs 3:31 (KJV)**

Though the Bible instructs us to not envy the oppressor nor choose any of his ways, many Christian businesspersons fail or become victims to the wiles of the enemy because they have not been obedient to this scripture. According to the American Heritage Dictionary, to envy is to have a feeling of discontentment and resentment aroused by desiring someone else's possessions or qualities, accompanied by a strong desire to have them for oneself.[1] In the context of this teaching, the oppressor is a nonbeliever or a believer who is not operating according to the will of God. This person is in a superior position and tends to use his or her influence or resources in ways that do not glorify the Lord. Why, you may ask, would someone envy another whose values are obviously contrary to his own, or who is operating contrary to the Word of God? The benefits of taking shortcuts and operating in an unscrupulous manner in business can be tempting; oftentimes, the greedy capitalist is envied because of his car, clothes, money, and influence. Sadly, this temptation affects many Christians. They find themselves envying even those who operate contrary to biblical values because they become enamored with their material wealth. People caught up in 'Keeping up with the Joneses' ignore the fact that an oppressor employs ungodly means (ways) to acquire the things he possesses. What we often fail to realize is that as long as we desire the things the oppressor has, we will end up choosing his ways, and that is essentially what this scripture is saying: if you envy the oppressor you will choose his ways. Some of the ways of the oppressor include lying, cheating, and intimidation. The key to not choosing the ways of the oppressor is to stop lusting after the benefits of the oppressor. Yes, reject the car, money, clothes, and influence. Now of course we need transportation and clothing,

BE Thought of the Day

What we often fail to realize is that as long as we desire the things the oppressor has, we will end up choosing his ways, and that is essentially what this scripture is saying: if you envy the oppressor you will choose his ways.

and in this culture we need money to purchase them. What is wrong with influence, you may ask? Nothing, inherently…for did not the Lord Himself say in Matthew 6:32 that He knows that we have need of things? He also said, "*…seek first his kingdom and his righteousness, and all these things will be given to you as well*" (Matthew 6:33). In His Word He states, "*Delight yourself in the LORD and he will give you the desires of your heart*" (Psalm 37:4). He further admonishes us: "*Do not wear yourself out to get rich*" (Proverbs 23:4) and "*Better a little with righteousness than much gain with injustice*" (Proverbs 16:8). In other words, if you are going to be a Biblical Entrepreneur, you must commit in your heart that unless you can operate a profitable business based on the Word of God and His principles, you will not be in business. You will not seek to succeed in business by any means necessary but rather, you will obey God by any means necessary. Therefore, you will reject the benefits of the oppressor and seek the benefits of God which does not preclude natural provision, but expands itself beyond that to include peace of mind and fulfillment.

BE Prayer of the Day

Father, I choose to delight in You and not to envy people in the world for I know that You are faithful to supply all my needs and give me life in abundance, in Jesus' name, Amen.

BE Application of the Day

- In what ways have you been envying the oppressor?
- Stop lusting after the oppressor's wealth and know that God is faithful and His blessings extend beyond financial profits.

_____

_____

_____

_____

_____

_____

_____

_____

_____

_____

_____

_____

_____

_____

_____

_____

- Reflect on these passages of scripture and explain how they relate to today's devotional: Proverbs 16:25 and Romans 1:18-32.

_____

_____

_____

_____

_____

_____

_____

_____

_____

_____

_____

_____

Day 32

BIBLICAL ENTREPRENEURSHIP VERSUS WORLDLY ENTREPRENEURSHIP

So I say, live by the Spirit, and you will not gratify the desires of the sinful nature. For the sinful nature desires what is contrary to the Spirit, and the Spirit what is contrary to the sinful nature. They are in conflict with each other, so that you do not do what you want.

Galatians 5:16 – 17

BIBLICAL ENTREPRENEURSHIP
1. **Uses spiritual gifts and skills**
2. **Business steward**
3. **Biblical profit**
4. **Ideas inspired by God**
5. **Directed by the Holy Spirit**
6. **Confidence in God**
7. **Motivated by love**
8. **Interdependent**
9. **Cooperative**
10. **Driven by Calling**
11. **Kingdom focus**
12. **Enjoys serving others**
13. **Follows God's methods**

WORLDY ENTREPRENEURSHIP
1. **Uses only natural skills**
2. **Business owner**
3. **Worldly profit**
4. **Self-motivated**
5. **Self-driven**
6. **Confidence in self**
7. **Motivated by money**
8. **Independent**
9. **Competitive**
10. **Driven by Career**
11. **Big business focus**
12. **Enjoys commanding others**
13. **Originates own methods**

ϨᎧ BE Thought of the Day

When business is operated improperly, using worldly ways and methods, the outcome is ultimately the following: Death, the works of the flesh are manifested, Lack of peace, Lack of fulfillment, Temporary rewards, Others suffer lack, Eternal punishment.

- *When business is operated properly using Biblical principles we can experience the following outcomes:*
    - Abundant Life
    - The fruit of the Spirit is manifested
    - Contentment
    - Fulfillment
    - Temporal and eternal rewards
    - None suffers lack
    - The Great Commission is fulfilled

- *When business is operated improperly, using worldly ways and methods, the outcome is ultimately the following:*
    - Death
    - The works of the flesh are manifested
    - Lack of peace
    - Lack of fulfillment
    - Temporary rewards
    - Others suffer lack
    - Eternal punishment

These benefits are not devoid of trials and persecutions. However, make a commitment today to reject the worldly approach to entrepreneurship and choose to be a Biblical Entrepreneur.

BE Prayer of the Day

Father, You are faithful to reward those who do business in a way that glorifies You. Help me to operate my business in a way that lines up with Your Word, in Jesus' name, Amen.

BE Application of the Day

- Examine your life as a businessperson.
- Have you been operating as a biblical or a worldly entrepreneur?
- Make the decision today to change your ways.

_____
_____
_____
_____
_____
_____
_____
_____
_____
_____
_____
_____
_____
_____
_____

- Reflect on these passages of scripture and explain how they relate to today's devotional: Psalm 112:5-10 and Luke 6:27-36.

_____
_____
_____
_____
_____
_____
_____
_____
_____
_____
_____
_____
_____
_____

Day 33

JOSEPH'S WILDERNESS

"Remember how the LORD your God led you all the way in the desert these forty years, to humble you and to test you in order to know what was in your heart, whether or not you would keep his commands."   **Deuteronomy 8:2**

Though Joseph was destined by God for greatness, he was not born ready for that greatness; he displayed youthful arrogance, was spoiled by his father, and was very naïve.

These traits are demonstrated by these key facts:
- He brought a bad report to his father about his brothers
- He was his father's favorite
- He boasted to his brothers and father about his dream in which he would rule over them

This is the account of Jacob.
Joseph, a young man of seventeen, was tending the flocks with his brothers, the sons of Bilhah and the sons of Zilpah, his father's wives, and he brought their father a bad report about them. Now Israel loved Joseph more than any of his other sons, because he had been born to him in his old age; and he made a richly ornamented robe for him. (Genesis 37:2-3).

Joseph had a dream, and when he told it to his brothers, they hated him all the more. He said to them, "Listen to this dream I had: We were binding sheaves of grain out in the field when suddenly my sheaf rose and stood upright, while your sheaves gathered around mine and bowed down to it." His brothers said to him, "Do you intend to reign over us? Will you actually rule us" And they hated him all the more because of his dream and what he had said. Then he had another dream, and he told it to his brothers. "Listen," he said, "I had another dream, and this time the sun and moon and eleven stars

> **℘ BE Thought of the Day**
>
> The wilderness is designed to perfect you not destroy you, to humble you not kill you, and to strengthen your relationship with God and not to steal it.

were bowing down to me." When he told his father as well as his brothers, his father rebuked him and said, "What is this dream you had? Will your mother and I and your brothers actually come and bow down to the ground before you?" (Genesis 37:5-10).

Because of this lack of readiness and maturity to walk in his divine calling, the Lord had to prepare and mature Joseph for his destiny. He had to go through what I call "The Wilderness Experience". The Wilderness Experience is a combination of trials, tests, and temptations, allowed by God, to perfect us and enable us to fulfill His will for our lives. Most of us believe we are ready the minute we receive the vision, especially if it is clear in our minds. However, the next several years will most likely be full of lessons to prepare us for our ultimate destiny. Since God works through human vessels and natural circumstances, in Joseph's case He used his jealous and spiteful brothers to send him through a process of trials and tests that would prepare him for his calling. Through this wilderness, Joseph experienced major trials and tests, along with several temptations. If you are going through the wilderness right now, remember this wilderness is designed to perfect you not destroy you, to humble you not kill you, and to strengthen your relationship with God and not to steal it. Allow the Holy Spirit to accomplish these things in you.

BE Prayer of the Day

Father, thank You that You are using my hard times to perfect me. I pray for the grace to allow You to do what You desire in my life no matter how much it costs me, in Jesus' name, Amen.

BE Application of the Day

- Have you gone through a wilderness? Are you going through one now?
- What lessons is God teaching you through your wilderness experience?

_____

_____

_____

_____

_____

_____

_____

_____

_____

_____

_____

_____

_____

- Reflect on these passages of scripture and explain how they relate to today's devotional: John 16:33 and James 1:2-4.

_____

_____

_____

_____

_____

_____

_____

_____

_____

_____

_____

_____

_____

_____

Day 34

THE PIT EXPERIENCE

Then they took him and cast him into a pit: and the pit was empty, there was no water in it.   **Genesis 37:24 (KJV)**

The pit is a hopeless state where only God's mercy can bring you through. The pit is designed to humble you. In the pit, you have no one to lean on or call upon but God. You feel as though you or your vision will surely die. The pit is that season of life when the circumstances we experience can cause hopelessness. During the pit experience, you have to pray and believe God for a miracle. If God does not intervene, it will be the end of your life or your business. God often intervenes in strange ways. He rescues us from death sometimes only to throw us into another difficult situation. During the pit experience, we learn that, *"man does not live on bread alone but on every word that comes from the mouth of the LORD"* (Deuteronomy 8:3).

"Here comes that dreamer!" they said to each other. "Come now, let's kill him and throw him into one of these cisterns and say that a ferocious animal devoured him. Then we'll see what comes of his dreams." When Reuben heard this, he tried to rescue him from their hands. "Let's not take his life," he said. "Don't shed any blood. Throw him into this cistern here in the desert, but don't lay a hand on him." Reuben said this to rescue him from them and take him back to his father. So when Joseph came to his brothers, they stripped him of his robe—the richly ornamented robe he was wearing- and they took him and threw him into the cistern. Now the cistern was empty; there was no water in it. As they sat down to eat their meal, they looked up and saw a caravan of Ishmaelites coming from Gilead. Their camels were loaded with spices, balm and myrrh, and they were on their way to take them down to Egypt. Judah said to his

> ✿ BE Thought of the Day
>
> During the pit experience, we learn that man shall not live by bread alone, but by every word that proceeds out of the mouth of God.

brothers, *"What will we gain if we kill our brother and cover up his blood? Come, let's sell him to the Ishmaelites and not lay our hands on him; after all, he is our brother, our own flesh and blood." His brothers agreed. So when the Midianite merchants came by, his brothers pulled Joseph up out of the cistern and sold him for twenty shekels of silver to the Ishmaelites, who took him to Egypt. When Reuben returned to the cistern and saw that Joseph was not there, he tore his clothes. He went back to his brothers and said, "The boy isn't there! Where can I turn now?" Then they got Joseph's robe, slaughtered a goat and dipped the robe in the blood. They took the ornamented robe back to their father and said, "We found this. Examine it to see whether it is your son's robe." He recognized it and said, "It is my son's robe! Some ferocious animal has devoured him. Joseph has surely been torn to pieces." Then Jacob tore his clothes, put on sackcloth and mourned for his son many days. All his sons and daughters came to comfort him, but he refused to be comforted. "No," he said, "in mourning will I go down to the grave to my son." So his father wept for him. Meanwhile, the Midianites sold Joseph in Egypt to Potiphar, one of Pharaoh's officials, the captain of the guard."* (Genesis 37:19-36).

Are you facing a pit experience? If so, *"lift up [your] eyes to the hills—where does [your] help come from? [Your] help comes from the LORD, the Maker of heaven and earth"* (Psalm 121:1-2). *"...he will never leave you nor forsake you"* (Deuteronomy 31:6). He will be with you until the end.

BE Prayer of the Day

Father, You are my help. In this tough time in my life I look to You for the strength I need to endure. Help me to lean on You and to learn all that You desire to teach me in this season, in Jesus' name, Amen.

BE Application of the Day

- Does it seem as though you or your business are in a pit?
- What message is God trying to get across to you?
- Although it may be difficult, allow Him to perfect you through this experience.

_____
_____
_____
_____
_____
_____
_____
_____
_____
_____
_____
_____
_____
_____

- Reflect on these passages of scripture and explain how they relate to today's devotional: Romans 5:1-5 and Hebrews 4:15-16.

_____
_____
_____
_____
_____
_____
_____
_____
_____
_____
_____
_____
_____
_____

Day 35

BUSINESS LESSONS FROM THE LIFE OF JOSEPH

"Remember how the LORD your God led you all the way in the desert these forty years, to humble you and to test you in order to know what was in your heart, whether or not you would keep his commands."

Deuteronomy 8:2

Like Joseph, most entrepreneurs are individuals destined for greatness, but not born prepared for it. They are dreamers, oftentimes with an unrealistic view of themselves. Many are arrogant, prideful, and feel as though they are the center of the universe. Their motive for being in business is usually self-centered; based on an internal drive for independence. A common theme for many entrepreneurs is "I want to start a business so that I can be my own boss." They do not realize that starting a business does not make you a boss but rather a servant. As an entrepreneur, you are God's steward, called to serve customers and your employees. Though most Christian entrepreneurs will profess to believe this and even practice it, the wilderness experience allows them to see if they really mean what they say.

All born-again believers who are called of God to carry out a great work must go through the wilderness. You have either gone through your wilderness, are going through it now, or you will go through it in the future. However, like Joseph, the wilderness is designed to perfect you and not destroy you. It is designed to bring you into a state of total dependency upon God so that He may exalt you and reveal to you the fullness of your destiny. Therefore, do not distain the trials and tests you have gone through, are going through, or will go through. Look at the lessons you can learn from them that will enable you to fulfill God's plan for your life.

🕊 BE Thought of the Day

Starting a business does not make you a boss but rather a servant.

"He humbled you, causing you to hunger and then feeding you with manna, which neither you nor your fathers had known, to teach you that man does not live on bread alone

but on every word that comes from the mouth of the LORD. Your clothes did not wear out and your feet did not swell during these forty years. Know then in your heart that as a man disciplines his son, so the LORD your God disciplines you." (Deuteronomy 8:3-5)

Our ultimate destiny is not our business or the job we have; those are mere instruments that God uses to enable us to fulfill our destiny. Our destiny rests in how we are using whatever God has blessed us with to conform to His image and likeness, and to be a witness for Him in the marketplace. The results should be that more souls come to know Jesus Christ as their personal Lord and Savior through our personal witness and our ministry. The Lord does not really care what type of business you start or even if you start one. He is concerned with whether or not you have used the talents that He placed under your care profitably because His instructions are "do business until I come" for He is coming back.

BE Prayer of the Day

Father, help me to view myself as the servant You have called me to be and give me the grace to live a life that is totally dependent on You, in Jesus' name, Amen.

BE Application of the Day

- What have been your motives for doing business?
- Have you been operating as a boss or a servant?
- Have you been despising your trials or allowing God to use them to perfect you?

_____

_____

_____

_____

_____

_____

_____

_____

_____

_____

_____

_____

_____

- Reflect on these passages of scripture and explain how they relate to today's devotional: Proverbs 13:24 and Hebrews 12:7-11.

_____

_____

_____

_____

_____

_____

_____

_____

_____

_____

_____

_____

_____

Day 36

JOSEPH'S DESTINY IS REVEALED

But God sent me ahead of you to preserve for you a remnant on earth and to save your lives by a great deliverance.   **Genesis 45:7**

When Joseph had his dream as a teenager, his interpretation was that he would rule over his brothers and parents and they would serve him. Joseph's immaturity caused him to define greatness as a position of lordship versus one of service. Jesus would later teach His disciples this lesson in Mark 10:35-45: *Jesus called them together and said, "You know that those who are regarded as rulers of the Gentiles lord it over them, and their high officials exercise authority over them. Not so with you. Instead, whoever wants to become great among you must be your servant, and whoever wants to be first must be slave of all. For even the Son of Man did not come to be served, but to serve, and to give his life as a ransom for many".*

Joseph's wrong attitude caused the Lord to take him through the wilderness experience. Once Joseph's attitude was corrected, the Lord could reveal his ultimate destiny to him; not lordship over his brothers, but service to them. What allowed Joseph to see his destiny was the fact that he forgave his brothers. Prior to the forgiveness, he was attempting to ensure his well-being as well as that of his younger brother, Benjamin. However, once he forgave, he realized that it was not just about him and his brother, but about his entire family; even those who had sold him into slavery.

> ℘ BE Thought of the Day
>
> Once Joseph was fully perfected, the Lord could reveal his ultimate destiny to him; not lordship over his brothers, but service to them.

Though Joseph saw himself as the center of the story, it was really never about him, but his brothers. More particularly, it was about Judah. Why Judah, you may ask? From the loins of Judah would come our Lord and Savior Jesus Christ. The Lord sent Joseph ahead to Egypt because He knew there was a famine coming, and He needed to protect the Seed, Jesus Christ our Savior. This Seed would take away the sins of the entire human race so that "whoever believes in Him shall not perish but have eternal life" (John 3:16). We can even see Christ manifested in Judah when he interceded on behalf of Benjamin by putting his own life on the line so that Benjamin would be saved. That act foreshadowed what was to come as Christ would come and lay down His life so that we might be saved. In that act, it was not Judah who was speaking, but Christ Himself.

BE Prayer of the Day

Father, You promised to forgive me if I forgive those who wrong me. Help me to forgive even those who've caused me great pain. Help me also to remember that You are the one in control and that my life is not about me, but about Your ultimate purpose, in Jesus' name, Amen.

BE Application of the Day

- Is there anyone you need to forgive?
- Have you been self-centered?
- Remember that it's not about you, but about the bigger picture God is working out.

_____
_____
_____
_____
_____
_____
_____
_____
_____
_____
_____
_____
_____

- Reflect on these passages of scripture and explain how they relate to today's devotional: Matthew 6:14-15 and Mark 9:33-35.

_____
_____
_____
_____
_____
_____
_____
_____
_____
_____
_____
_____
_____
_____

Day 37

HOW JOSEPH IDENTIFIED OPPORTUNITIES IN EGYPT

"Come, let's sell him to the Ishmaelites and not lay our hands on him; after all, he is our brother, our own flesh and blood." His brothers agreed. **Genesis 37:27**

Identifying Opportunity is recognizing when God's timing meets preparation. Though Joseph was sold into slavery, the Lord used many circumstances and experiences to prepare him for the time he would be steward over Egypt. Joseph was sold into slavery under Potiphar; his work as a slave gave him the experience he needed to be a steward over food and household goods. Joseph gained leadership experience while in prison. The prison keeper promoted him to a leadership position. To ensure that he would be prepared for the prestigious position of governor over Egypt, Joseph's character and faithfulness were tested while he was a steward in Potiphar's house and as head of the prisoners in the King's prison. Joseph saw the faithfulness of God in his life, which gave him courage at the risk of his own life to give the credit to God before Pharaoh (who was viewed by the Egyptians as a god-like figure). Joseph's experiences humbled him and enabled God to exalt him in due time.

Like Joseph, God has allowed you to go through many circumstances and experiences, some positive and some negative. Keep in mind that these experiences are preparing you for opportunities that God will set before you. According to Romans 8:28, *"And we know that in all things God works for the good of those who love him, who have been called according to his purpose."* Be assured and know that if you love God and remain in His will for your life, you are called according to His purpose. It is possible that you are reading this devotional because you want to make sure

> ❧ BE Thought of the Day
>
> Your experiences are preparing you for opportunities that God will set before you.

you please Him as you start or operate your business. Although you may be unsure of the purpose for which God is preparing you, be faithful and diligent in all of your responsibilities, such as your job, ministry, or business. These are the ways God prepares His leaders. Whenever something negative happens to you, through no fault of your own, or due to your own poor choices, determine to see it as a way that God is preparing you for an opportunity to serve Him and His people in the future.

BE Prayer of the Day

Father, as You are preparing me for the opportunities You have in store for me, I ask that You help me to be diligent and faithful with the responsibilities I currently have, in Jesus' name, Amen.

BE Application of the Day

- What is God using to prepare you for the opportunities that are ahead?
- Are you being faithful with all that you currently have?
- In what areas could you increase your faithfulness?

_____

_____

_____

_____

_____

_____

_____

_____

_____

_____

_____

_____

_____

_____

- Reflect on these passages of scripture and explain how they relate to today's devotional: 1 Samuel 17: 34-37 and Luke 16:12.

_____

_____

_____

_____

_____

_____

_____

_____

_____

_____

_____

_____

_____

_____

Day 38

FOR GOD SO LOVED THE WORLD

For God so loved the world that he gave his one and only Son, that whoever believes in him shall not perish but have eternal life.   **John 3:16**

John 3:16 could be stated this way: for God so loved sinful humanity that He started a global enterprise called Operation Rescue, Inc. This enterprise had one product called the Gospel. God assigned His only begotten son, Jesus, to serve as the CEO. Jesus' goal was to recruit and train men who would lead this new enterprise, and their mission was to seek and save the lost. How could a Holy God love sinful humanity? Does He not hate sin? God saw humanity's potential if only someone could rescue it from its current state. He was so excited about that potential that He forgot all reason, and faith and love kicked in to make it a reality. God knew that not everyone would accept His product and not everyone who does accept it will appreciate it. He rejoiced knowing that if only one person accepts and appreciates His product it would all have been worth it. He did His market research and knew that enough people would accept His product to keep the business profitable. Then again, since He owns everything, He could not lose. His love compelled Him to believe in humanity more than it could believe in itself. What is your motivation for being in business? Our motivation is what fuels our passion for the business. It drives us and inspires us to defy logic and move by faith to make the impossible possible. Our motivation helps us overcome the difficult times of business, it helps us overcome fear to ensure that we will not fail. Are you motivated by love or by money?

Here are a few things to consider.

Motivated by Love:
Suffers long with the customer
Patient with the customer
Kind to the customer
Humble before the customer
Is not rude to the customer

> ℘ BE Thought of the Day
>
> Our motivation ... drives us and inspires us to defy logic and move by faith to make the impossible possible. Our motivation helps us overcome the difficult times of business, it helps us overcome fear to ensure that we will not fail.

Seeks the best interest of the customer
Is not easily provoked by the customer
Thinks no evil of the customer
Rejoices in the truth about the customer
Bears all things with the customer
Believes all things for the customer
Hopes all things for the customer
Endures all things with the customer

Motivated by Money:
Not willing to suffer for the customer
Impatient with the customer
Unkind to the customer
Exhibits pride before the customer
Obnoxious to the customer
Seeks the best interest of the company
Irritated by the customer
Thinks evil of the customer
Gossips about the customer
Is unwilling to bear the customer's burden
Has no faith in the customer
Loses hope for the customer
Not able to endure with the customer

When your motivation is money, the only thing that can help you love the customer is money. The problem with money is that it is temporal and you can never have enough of it. Consider the fact that God owns everything and has nothing else to gain. Since God is motivated purely by love, He has given us dominion over the works of His hands and has put all things under our feet. We therefore have nothing else to gain since all things have been put under our feet. We can focus on loving our customers and not money, trusting that our God will add all things unto us.

BE Prayer of the Day

Father, I ask You to purify my motives. Help me to be motivated by love, just as You are. May that motivation drive my relationships and my business, in Jesus' name, Amen.

BE Application of the Day

- What characteristics do you notice in yourself?
- What is your motivation?
- How can you change your motivation to ensure that it lines up with God's?

_____
_____
_____
_____
_____
_____
_____
_____
_____
_____
_____
_____
_____
_____

- Reflect on these passages of scripture and explain how they relate to today's devotional: Proverbs 10:12 and 1 Corinthians 10:24.

_____
_____
_____
_____
_____
_____
_____
_____
_____
_____
_____
_____
_____

Day 39

UNCONDITIONAL LOVE

And now these three remain: faith, hope and love. But the greatest of these is love.

I Corinthians 13:13

There are three types of love found in the Greek language to which the Bible makes reference: **Eros** love, a love that is expressed through physical and sexual desire; **Philos** love, an esteem and affection found in casual friendship; **Agape** love, love based on the deliberate choice of the one who loves rather than the worthiness of the one who is loved. This type of love goes against our natural instinct and is best demonstrated by the love that Christ expressed for us by dying on the cross for our sins. Biblical Entrepreneurs are called to express this type of love to their customers, employees, and all of those they encounter in business. This type of love is called unconditional love, a love that is expressed without conditions or expectations. Agape is a love that is undeserved and could not be purchased by the recipient. It is a love that is sacrificial and, therefore, Christ-like. Loving your customers this way will increase your bottom line and make you a more effective witness for Christ before them. Loving your employees this way will increase their fulfillment on the job and their loyalty to the company. How does one express this type of love, especially to people who are undeserving and unappreciative?

The following four points will help you express unconditional love:

> **BE Thought of the Day**
>
> ...if you focus on individuals' actions you will find many reasons not to love them since they are imperfect beings. Raise your love above what they may or may not do to you.

1. **Make Christ the object of your love and not the person** – As you express love to individuals focus on Christ and let the individual be the mere beneficiary of your love for Christ.

2. **Put your love above their actions** – If you focus on individuals' actions, you

153

will find many reasons not to love them since they are imperfect beings. Raise your love above what they may or may not do to you.

3. **Remember that Christ died for them** – For God so loved the world that He sent Jesus to die for sinners like you and me. No matter how bad individuals behave, just remember the price that Christ paid for them. Would you want to be the reason they do not embrace the Gospel?

4. **Christ commands you to love** – Jesus was asked by someone what the greatest commandment is. His response was, "*Love the Lord your God with all your heart and with all your soul and with all your mind. This is the first and greatest commandment. And the second is like it: Love your neighbor as yourself. All the Law and the Prophets hang on these two commandments*" (Matthew 22:37-40). Your neighbor could be your customer or your employee.

Since this type of love is so demanding, are there any benefits to it? Yes there are. Some of the key benefits of expressing this type of love include:

- You are being obedient to the Father
- It never fails
- It conquers fear
- It enhances your communication
- It is profitable
- It enhances your self-worth
- You are emulating Christ

BE Prayer of the Day

Father, thank You for the unconditional love You have for me. Help me to begin to demonstrate this love to those around me, in Jesus' name, Amen.

BE Application of the Day

- Is your love toward others conditional?
- In what ways can you begin to express unconditional love?

_____

_____

_____

_____

_____

_____

_____

_____

_____

_____

_____

_____

_____

_____

_____

- Reflect on these passages of scripture and explain how they relate to today's devotional: Matthew 5:38-48 and Acts 7:59-60.

_____

_____

_____

_____

_____

_____

_____

_____

_____

_____

_____

_____

_____

Day 40

EMBRACING YOUR PRIVILEGE

Your attitude should be the same as that of Christ Jesus: Who, being in very nature God, did not consider equality with God something to be grasped, but made himself nothing, taking the very nature of a servant, being made in human likeness.

Philippians 2:5-7

Privilege is defined as a special advantage or immunity not embraced by all, or a right reserved exclusively for a particular person or group. Throughout the history of mankind, there has always been a group of people who were more privileged than others. In many situations there are several individuals who enjoy certain privileges based on their position, their pedigree, or their personal accomplishments. Having groups or individuals who are privileged is not something that was invented by man. Throughout the Bible we see groups and individuals who enjoy special advantages or rights because of their relationship with God. Our Lord and Savior Jesus Christ came as one who was privileged. He enjoyed special advantages as the only begotten Son of God, being God in the flesh and having all powers under His command. The key to privilege is not the privilege itself but rather how you use the privilege. Jesus did not deny nor reject His privilege but used it to fulfill the will of His father. He was not ashamed of it but rather through meekness, called upon His privilege to achieve the mission He was given to accomplish.

There are many believers who find themselves privileged because of the family they are born into, the country they are from, or just by the mere fact that they have accomplished success in their vocation or business. However, they are ashamed or feel guilty that they are able to enjoy certain privileges or rights that others do not have. Like Jesus Christ, you must not be ashamed of your privilege but rather embrace it

> **𝔊 BE Thought of the Day**
>
> Jesus did not deny nor reject His privilege but used it to fulfill the will of His father. He was not ashamed of it but rather through meekness, called upon His privilege to achieve the mission He was given to accomplish.

and seek the Lord as to how you ought to use that privilege to fulfill His will in the earth realm. By the grace of God I grew up privileged, the son of a successful businesswoman and politician. My family enjoyed the privileges of the ruling class of my country. Because of this privilege, I was able to come to the United States and enjoyed a certain education early in my development; I had certain exposure to business and government that the average person does not have. I enjoyed relationships with individuals who inspired me to believe in myself and pursue my dreams. With this privilege came a responsibility; thank God I had a mother who taught us about the responsibility of privilege. Your privilege is not so that you can enjoy the finer things of life, but rather so that you can be of service to others. My coming to Christ brought an eternal dimension to this concept. Every child of God is privileged. The Bible tells us that we are joint heirs with Christ, we are kings and priests, and God has given us stewardship over the works of His hands. What a privilege! Someone more powerful than my mother, richer than Bill Gates, and wiser than Einstein, has made us joint heirs with His only begotten Son. He has made us to be kings and priests, meaning that we are little rulers in our own rights and can come to Him boldly for spiritual matters. He also placed His resources at our disposal. Wow! Thank God for men and women of God who have historically used their privilege to accomplish God's will in the earth. Should your business become a financial success so that your children and grandchildren enjoy the privileges I enjoyed, make sure they understand the responsibility of privilege and its eternal implications, so they may build upon your legacy to continue to advance the will of God in the earth.

BE Prayer of the Day

Father, thank You for the privileges You have given me. Help me to embrace them and to use them for Your honor, in Jesus' name, Amen.

BE Application of the Day

- Embrace your privilege and understand the awesome responsibility that comes with it.
- Do not be ashamed nor feel guilty about it. Rather, ask God why He privileged you and how you ought to use that privilege for His glory.

_____

_____

_____

_____

_____

_____

_____

_____

_____

_____

_____

_____

_____

- Reflect on these passages of scripture and explain how they relate to today's devotional: Deuteronomy 7:6 and 1 Peter 2:9.

_____

_____

_____

_____

_____

_____

_____

_____

_____

_____

_____

_____

_____

_____

_____

Notes

Notes

Scripture References

GENESIS

Then they took him and cast him into a pit. And the pit was empty; there was no water in it. **Genesis 37:24 KJV (Day 34)**

"Come, let's sell him to the Ishmaelites and not lay our hands on him; after all, he is our brother, our own flesh and blood." His brothers agreed. **Genesis 37:27 (Day 37)**

So Pharaoh asked them, "Can we find anyone like this man, one in whom is the spirit of God?" Then Pharaoh said to Joseph, "Since God has made all this known to you, there is no one so discerning and wise as you. You shall be in charge of my palace, and all my people are to submit to your orders. Only with respect to the throne will I be greater than you." So Pharaoh said to Joseph, "I hereby put you in charge of the whole land of Egypt." Then Pharaoh took his signet ring from his finger and put it on Joseph's finger. He dressed him in robes of fine linen and put a gold chain around his neck. He had him ride in a chariot as his second-in-command, and men shouted before him, "Make way!" Thus he put him in charge of the whole land of Egypt. **Genesis 41:38-43 (Day 3)**

But God sent me ahead of you to preserve for you a remnant on earth and to save your lives by a great deliverance. **Genesis 45:7 (Day 36)**

EXODUS

See that you make them according to the pattern shown you on the mountain. **Exodus 25:40 (Day 8)**

DEUTERONOMY

"Remember how the LORD your God led you all the way in the desert these forty years, to humble you and to test you in order to know what was in your heart, whether or not you would keep his commands." **Deuteronomy 8:2 (Day 33, Day 35)**

Be careful that you do not forget the LORD your God, failing to observe his commands, his laws and his decrees that I am giving you this day. **Deuteronomy 8:11 (Day 27)**

But thou shalt remember the LORD thy God: for it is he that giveth thee power to get wealth, that he may establish his covenant which he sware unto thy fathers, as it is this day. **Deuteronomy 8:18 KJV (Day 26)**

1 SAMUEL
But now your kingdom will not endure; the LORD has sought out a man after his own heart and appointed him leader of his people, because you have not kept the LORD's command. **I Samuel 13:14 (Day 25)**

2 KINGS
She went and told the man of God, and he said, "Go, sell the oil and pay your debts. You and your sons can live on what is left." **2 Kings 4:7 (Day 15)**

PSALMS
O LORD, our Lord, how majestic is your name in all the earth! You have set your glory above the heavens. From the lips of children and infants you have ordained praise because of your enemies, to silence the foe and the avenger. When I consider your heavens, the work of your fingers, the moon and the stars, which you have set in place, what is man that you are mindful of him, the son of man that you care for him? You made him a little lower than the heavenly beings and crowned him with glory and honor. You made him ruler over the works of your hands; you put everything under his feet: all flocks and herds, and the beasts of the field, the birds of the air, and the fish of the sea, all that swim the paths of the seas. O LORD, our Lord, how majestic is your name in all the earth! **Psalm 8:1-9 (Day 6)**

Who may ascend the hill of the Lord? Who may stand in his holy place? He who has clean hands and a pure heart, who does not lift up his soul to an idol or swear by what is false. **Psalm 24:3-4 (Day 2)**

PROVERBS
"Envy thou not the oppressor, and choose none of his ways." **Proverbs 3:31 KJV (Day 31)**

"Where there is no vision, the people perish: but he that keepeth the law, happy is he". **Proverbs 29:18 KJV (Day 28)**

"Who can find a virtuous woman? For her worth is far above rubies." **Proverbs 31:10 KJV (Day 17)**

JEREMIAH
Before I formed you in the womb I knew you, before you were born I set you apart; I appointed you as a prophet to the nations." **Jeremiah 1:5 (Day 29)**

MATTHEW
Then Joseph her husband, being a just man, and not willing to make her a public example, was minded to put her away privily. **Matthew 1:19 KJV (Day 18)**

Blessed are those who hunger and thirst for righteousness, for they will be filled. **Matthew 5:6 (Day 10)**

Jesus turned and said to Peter, "Get behind me, Satan! You are a stumbling block to me; you do not have in mind the things of God, but the things of men." **Matthew 16:23 (Day 20)**

Then he that had received the five talents went and traded with the same, and made them other five talents. And likewise he that had received two, he also gained other two." **Matthew 25:16-17 KJV (Day 19)**

"After a long time the master of those servants returned and settled accounts with them." **Matthew 25:19 (Day 22)**

The man who had received the five talents brought the other five. "Master," he said, "you entrusted me with five talents. See, I have gained five more" … The man with the two talents also came. "Master," he said, "you entrusted me with two talents; see, I have gained two more." **Matthew 25:20, 22 (Day 21)**

Then the man who had received the one talent came. "Master," he said, "I knew that you are a hard man, harvesting where you have not sown and gathering where you have not scattered seed. So I was afraid and went out and hid your talent in the ground. See, here is what belongs to you." **Matthew 25:24-25 (Day 23)**

Take the talent from him and give it to the one who has the ten talents…And throw that worthless servant outside, into the darkness, where there will be weeping and gnashing of teeth. **Matthew 25: 28, 30 (Day 24)**

LUKE
…Then Jesus said to Simon, "Don't be afraid from now on you will catch men." So they pulled their boats up on shore, left everything and followed him. **Luke 5:10-11 (Day 1)**

Suppose one of you wants to build a tower. Will he not first sit down and estimate the cost to see if he has enough money to complete it? **Luke 14:28 (Day 4)**

JOHN
For God so loved the world that he gave his one and only Son, that whoever believes in him shall not perish but have eternal life. **John 3:16 (Day 38)**

ROMANS
No, in all these things we are more than conquerors through Him who loved us. **Romans 8:37 (Day 14)**

1 CORINTHIANS
And now these three remain: faith, hope and love. But the greatest of these is love. **I Corinthians 13:13 (Day 39)**

If there is no resurrection of the dead, then not even Christ has been raised. And if Christ has not been raised, our preaching is useless and so is your faith. **I Corinthians 15:13-14 (Day 12)**

2 CORINTHIANS
…My Grace is sufficient for you, for my power is made perfect in weakness. **2 Corinthians 12:9 (Day 16)**

GALATIANS
So I say, live by the Spirit, and you will not gratify the desires of the sinful nature. For the sinful nature desires what is contrary to the Spirit, and the Spirit what is contrary to the sinful nature. They are in conflict with each other, so that you do not do what you want. **Galatians 5:16 – 17 (Day 32)**

PHILIPPIANS
Your attitude should be the same as that of Christ Jesus: Who, being in very nature God, did not consider equality with God something to be grasped, but made himself nothing, taking the very nature of a servant, being made in human likeness. **Philippians 2:5-7 (Day 40)**

Do not be anxious about anything, but in everything, by prayer and petition, with thanksgiving, present your requests to God. And the peace of God, which transcends all understanding, will guard your hearts and your minds in Christ Jesus. **Philippians 4:6-7 (Day 5)**

1 TIMOTHY
"But godliness with contentment is great gain" **I Timothy 6:6 (Day 7)**

JAMES
My brethren, count it all joy when ye fall into divers temptations; knowing this, that the trying of your faith worketh patience. But let patience have her perfect work, that ye may be perfect and entire, wanting nothing. **James 1:2-4 KJV (Day 9)**

"But let patience have her perfect work, that ye may be perfect and entire, wanting nothing". **James 1:4 KJV (Day 11)**

If any of you lacks wisdom, he should ask God, who gives generously to all without finding fault, and it will be given to him. **James 1:5 (Day 30)**

REVELATION
With a mighty voice he shouted: Fallen! Fallen is Babylon the Great! She has become a home for demons and a haunt for every evil spirit, a haunt for every unclean and detestable bird! **Revelation 18:2 (Day 13)**

Bibliography

[1] "envy." *The American Heritage® Dictionary of the English Language, Fourth Edition*. Houghton Mifflin Company, 2004. 14 Feb. 2008. <Dictionary.com http://dictionary.reference.com/browse/ envy>.

Note From The Author

Congratulations, you have just completed the 40–day challenge. Please write and let me how it has impacted your spiritual and business life. E-mail your letters to ptsague@nehemiahproject.org or mail them to 10715 Brink Road, Germantown, MD 20876. Thank you.

Overview of NPIM Inc.

Nehemiah Project International Ministries Inc. (NPIM) was founded in 1999 by Gina and Patrice Tsague. NPIM is a non-profit, tax exempt business training and support service organization that works in partnership with organizations and individuals to develop and operate marketplace ministries that equip individuals and families with biblical entrepreneurial training.

NPIM offers a proprietary certificate business course called "Biblical Entrepreneurship" that provides a strong mix of core business concepts and biblical principles. Some of the courses offered include Principles of Biblical Entrepreneurship (BE I), Practices of Biblical Entrepreneurship (BE II), and Planning a Biblically-based Business (BE III). Most graduates of the program successfully began and continue to operate small and medium-sized businesses here in the United States and in Cameroon, Central Africa. The largest business to enroll and complete the course is worth over $12 million dollars. To date, NPIM has trained over 1200 students in the United States and Cameroon, Central Africa. NPIM also offers alumni support services to its graduates.

Our mission is to equip and empower people to steward God's resources through biblically based entrepreneurial training thereby helping them fulfill God's plan for their lives.

Our vision is to be a leader in marketplace ministry training and business support services to serve at least 10,000 people a year by 2013.

Objectives:
To lead individuals to salvation through our witness
To transform lives through biblically based entrepreneurial training
To develop successful Biblical Entrepreneurship businesses through business support

NPIM defines a successful business as a business that meets the following five criteria:

1. Business is a tool to fulfill God's plan for the steward (s).
2. Products and services honor the Lord Jesus Christ.
3. Management is a witness to the Lord Jesus Christ.
4. Business provides for the natural needs of the Biblical Entrepreneur and his or her family.
5. Business contributes to the advancement of the Kingdom of God by creating jobs, making financial contributions, and through professional expertise.

To enroll in the program or for more information on how to partner with NPIM to bring the Biblical Entrepreneurship Certificate program into your community or organization contact us toll free at 1-877-916-1180 or visit our website www.nehemiahproject.org.

CPSIA information can be obtained at www.ICGtesting.com
Printed in the USA
BVOW07s2019171114

375515BV00002B/80/P

9 781434 382368